ROY

ROY

GOING FOR BROKE

ANDREW SYMONDS

WITH STEPHEN GRAY

Hardie Grant Books

This edition published in 2007
First published in 2006,
reprinted in 2007 by
Hardie Grant Books
85 High Street
Prahran, Victoria 3181, Australia
www.hardiegrant.com.au

Cataloguing-in-Publication data is available from the
National Library of Australia.

ISBN 978 1 74066 580 3

Cover design by Nada Backovic
Internal design by Pigs Might Fly Productions
Typesetting by Kirby Jones
Colour photograph section designed by Lou Kubicki
Statistical information courtesy Ross Dundas, Ric Finlay and Cricinfo
Printed and bound in Australia by McPherson's Printing Group

10 9 8 7 6 5 4 3 2 1

To Mum, Dad, Nick and Louise –
my family, my strength.

YOU RIPPER ROY

With the comfort of wickets – three scalps of the Bok
He strode to the centre – he needed a knock
He looked to his partner – his dreadlocks a swishing
And Haydos said, 'Simmo – it's time we went fishing'
The white-lipped assassin then brandished his rod
He baited his hook and replied with a nod
With a six to get started, he signalled his ploy
And I whispered ambitiously, 'You ripper Roy.'

He fed off the frenzy – the spinners inviting
His rod kept on casting – the big ones kept biting
His shoulders unfolded – the onslaught was violent
Six monster snapper! The critics went silent
He flailed 'em, he nailed 'em, he scaled 'em as well
His fifty was fitting – the straight one off Nel
With a sigh of relief and a quiet tear of joy
I hugged my three kids and screamed, 'YOU RIPPER ROY!'

They towered like troubadours deadly defiant
The white-lipped assassin and Haydos the Giant
Bowlers once dominant cowered in fear
He came and he saw and he saved his career
To murder the seed with a flurry of wood
To do for his crest what we knew that he could
His wicketing war dance – his 'seek and destroy'
And the mob at the G chanted, 'You ripper Roy.'

Fate marks a moment in everyone's life
The tide turns at dusk and the big fish are rife
Instinct befriends you and confidence grows
Talent takes over and everything flows
Where to from here? Well, with him, who's to say?
The ocean is deep and the fella can play
For now let's acknowledge the dream of a boy
And the day he fulfilled it … 'You ripper Roy!'

Rupert McCall,
29 December 2005

CONTENTS

PROLOGUE 1

1 MY START IN LIFE 7

2 THE NORTH 21

3 THE GREAT OUTDOORS 37

4 WHY 'ROY'? 49

5 RUNNING WITH THE BULLS 59

6 THE MOTHER COUNTRY COMES CALLING 65

7 THE ROAD TO ABERGAVENNY 79

8 A PRETTY GOOD IMPRESSION 87

9 SALT AND PEPPER 97

10 SURVIVAL INSTINCTS 105

11 THE BIG SWITCH 121

12 THE WORLD CUP 131

13 THE TIN MAN AND THE BAGGY GREEN 147

14 CARDIFF 167

15 PINK GALAHS MIGHT FLY 179

16 BLOOD IN THE WATER 195

17 GET YOUR MOTOR RUNNING 211

18 THE 2006/07 ASHES SERIES 221

19 MY GOLDFIELD ASHES XI 233

ACKNOWLEDGMENTS 244

PHOTOGRAPHY CREDITS 248

PROLOGUE

Pulling a pair of sports socks onto sweaty feet when you're in a hurry isn't the easiest thing to do. Especially when there are nerves involved. And it's the opening game of the 2003 World Cup. And there's a three-pronged Pakistani pace attack out there revelling in the conditions. And Australia has lost two wickets in two balls and you're up next. And you were the last player selected for the squad … Stop me if this sounds like one of those dreams where you front up for a job interview wearing just your jocks.

As it turned out, what could have been a nightmare was actually one for the dreamers. But how I got to that players' room, fighting a losing battle with a pair of socks, is a story that even I still have trouble believing. The World Cup was the biggest moment of my cricketing career and just being selected to help defend the 1999 title was achievement enough. At the time most people reckoned I was dead-set the luckiest bloke in the country to be anywhere near the Wanderers Stadium in Johannesburg.

A month earlier, my old mate Jimmy 'Mahbo' Maher and I had had smiles like split watermelons. Along with Brad 'Barney' Hogg (so called because he sounds like Barney from *The Simpsons*), we'd scored the three spots widely tipped to be up for grabs in the 15-man international squad. Mahbo and I did our media conference together while training with Australia 'A' in Melbourne and, always up to speed with how the State cricketers were travelling, Mahbo rattled off a dozen or so contenders that could well have got our gigs. He meant it genuinely, and it made me sit up a bit straighter and think, 'Geez, *I'm* going to the World Cup.'

My next thought was: 'And you know what, you really don't deserve it.'

Not surprisingly, the media agreed and weren't all that flattering the next day. I couldn't blame them. I didn't pick the team but I was rapt to be in it: without putting too fine a point on it, this was my last chance. I'd already considered chucking cricket in six months prior, so going to the World Cup – the absolute pinnacle of the game – meant I had one last shot. The old adage goes that if you give a man a fish, he'll eat for a day, but if you teach him how to fish, he'll eat forever. Well, in a cricketing sense, I'd been taught well enough, but the fish were scarce and I was getting hungry.

◄█▉█►

By the time we arrived in South Africa, some of the old confidence had returned. I was physically strong and, going on past experience, that's when I was most likely to get it right on the field. We started off at Potchefstroom, a nice little town about 120 kilometres from

Johannesburg, and had the option of spending our downtime at a camping resort on the nearby Mooi River. Mooi translates as 'pretty', and pretty it certainly was. The fish were biting hard from the outset – a good omen, surely – and the fly-fishermen among us were stoked. By day two I'd landed the best catch of the tour, a yellowfish that was close to four pounds.

But it wasn't all beer and skittles: Michael Bevan was injured and Darren 'Boof' Lehmann was serving a five-match suspension for his outburst against the Sri Lankans during the VB Series back home. The only upside was that it meant Mahbo and I had a good chance of getting a run. After relocating to our Johannesburg hotel the morning of 10 February, we had a training session at the Wanderers Stadium. Later that day, feeling pretty relaxed, I got a call to head to one of the suites for a 6 pm meeting. This wasn't scheduled as far as I could recall, but knowing coach John 'Buck' Buchanan's love of meetings and my dodgy memory, I just assumed it had gone in one ear and out the other.

When I arrived at the suite, everyone was there – Shane Warne was the last one in. As soon as a very serious Warney took the stage and began, 'Boys, I've got something to tell you ...', my mind started racing. For some reason I thought he was going to retire, but that all changed when he dropped the bombshell: he'd tested positive to a banned 'substance' and would be withdrawing from the tournament immediately. He was understandably devastated, both for himself and the team, and watching the tears run down his cheeks hammered home to every one of us in that room that our World Cup campaign was sick before a single ball had been bowled.

I was furious, but couldn't really tell whether I was angry with Warney for getting caught, angry at the system that, for all I knew, could have been out to 'get' a mate, or angry at what it meant for our

World Cup hopes. Perhaps it was all of the above, or none. I didn't think Warney was a cheat but he'd taken the wrong thing and rules were rules.

We were really nervous on the bus to the ground the next day, and it didn't let up once we got there: you could have heard a pin drop in the dressing room. The jokers – and I'm one of them – weren't chirping up, so I tried to crack a few, but they didn't go far.

Then we lost the toss. And in the blink of an eye, we were in deep: Wasim Akram had his wicked way and Adam Gilchrist was out for one after just two overs before Matthew Hayden and Ricky Ponting dug in.

I'd begun the innings reclining in the players' area, wearing thongs, strides and a training T-shirt, but before you could say six and out, Haydos and Damien Martyn had fallen to Wassie in consecutive balls and I found myself downstairs wrestling with those bloody socks …

When I finally got them on, I couldn't find my thighpad, and you really don't want to go thighpad-less against Wassie and the boys. I turned the room upside down and lo and behold, there it was – in my hand – though I still don't remember where I found it. With the adrenaline starting to surge, I began the mental checklist:

Bat? Check.

Pads? Check.

Gloves? Check.

Box? Double check.

Inners. Two lefts. Bugger. Another rummage saw me confidently pull on two right-handers before I found a pair that I could actually wear. Okay.

Helmet? Yep.

Zinc? Yep.

Bat? Still with me.

Hands? Still shaking.

I charged back up to the viewing area, plonked down in the chair, took a deep breath … and looked up to see Mahbo edge one off Waqar.

That was it – I was out there.

CHAPTER 1

MY START IN LIFE

One of the best things about me being adopted was that I always knew. It was never this big secret that only came out when someone had had a few too many. Nor was there any trauma. Since as far back as I can remember, Mum and Dad told me I was their special little boy who they chose. They must know more about my birth parents, but frankly, I've never felt the urge to push them on it. I don't feel there's something missing in my life, I've no desire to 'rediscover my roots', and I don't spend time imagining what my biological parents might be like, or whether I've got another set of brothers or sisters. If someone contacted me out of the blue saying they were my mother or father, the first thing I'd say is, 'No, you're not – my Mum and Dad live down the road.' Beyond that, I can't be certain what I'd do, but I'm pretty sure I wouldn't be diving down the phone line to hug someone. I'd probably be more worried about how Mum and Dad would react.

In the backyard, aged two.

My younger brother, Nick, and little sister, Louise, aren't adopted but we treat each other as equals in every sense, even if we look different. I'm lucky in that we're as close now as when we were baiting hooks on one of our endless summer holidays, or collecting furry caterpillars to take back to camp (I should have known better, but poor old Nick just went along with what his big brother was doing ... I reckon we itched for days). I mightn't see them as often these days due to the fact we're all doing different things but, like most families, we've still got a tight bond.

I've met other adoptees but haven't felt any special kinship or link with them because we share a similar history. I've either liked them or not – it's been because of who they were, not because of where they came from or how they ended up where they are today. It's always been that way for me. I was given every opportunity as a kid and I've had an incredible life so far. I can't imagine it could get any better by poking around in someone else's business. This attitude probably won't get me a start on *Oprah* or *Dr Phil* but I think I'll survive just the same.

◼◼▮▮▶

I'm sometimes asked whether I consider myself 'black' or 'white', but the real answer is that I'm just me. Perhaps the confusion surrounding someone who is of 'mixed race' means that people might think there's a 50 per cent chance of being wrong. Well, in this case I'll use some of the famous Symonds maths ability and say there's probably a 100 per cent chance of being wrong! But you can't blame people for being curious or for speculating. Over the years I've heard some beauties: growing up as a kid in North Queensland, some thought I was Aboriginal or from the Torres Strait; another rumour about my origins (which I share with rugby star Wendell Sailor) was that I was either Clive Lloyd's or Viv Richards' 'love child'. Sorry folks, but my story has its beginnings in England, on the other side of the world.

To get to where I ended up – in the arms of Ken and Barbara Symonds, and eventually living in Australia – needs a bit of background. In fact, Australia plays a small but pivotal

With Mum, aged ten months.

role in my Dad's past: his father, Wally Symonds, had flown in the English Fleet Air Arm during World War II and, after the war, he decided to make a fresh start 'down under' with his new wife, Rita. It would have meant a move from one coastal community at Great Yarmouth in Norfolk, on the east coast of England, to another in Fremantle in Western Australia – a big shift back in those days.

As the details of the move were being finalised in late 1945, the couple found out that they were expecting their first child, my Dad. His impending arrival was enough to make Wally change his mind, and the grand plan was scrapped. Ken Symonds was born in 1946 and the family settled in Norfolk, in the village of Gorleston-on-Sea.

Dad will tell you that his love of cricket, and consequently my immersion in the sport, was almost a foregone conclusion: as treasurer of the local cricket club, Wally was heavily into the game and passed down his love to his son. The pair would rise at 4 am in the middle of winter, hunker down beside the freshly stoked fire and listen to a crackly wireless broadcasting the Ashes being played in

Australia. Dad's exposure to cricket was constant. He went to school with a member of the Edrich clan and knew that great cricketing family well, and was a decent player in the Norfolk Alliance League. If it weren't for a romance with a French girl when he was about 18, he might well have gone a whole lot further. Picked for a County Colts team, he declined the invitation as he was more interested in heading to the Continent to meet his mademoiselle. You might guess that this decision was not welcomed by his father and, as is often the case with these things, the selectors didn't come knocking again. As it turns out, it was a double whammy because the relationship ended a few months later.

Thankfully, a move to Cheltenham in 1967 to study teaching brought Dad into contact with Barbara Hemming, the woman who would become my mum. She was studying to be a home economics teacher in nearby Gloucester and the pair met and fell in love in September of Dad's second year. They got engaged on Valentine's Day in 1969 but shortly after, Dad had to spend six months studying in Paris, where Mum tells me his meagre allowance went largely towards a phone call home to her every day. It was worth every penny though, and they married in August 1970. Mum admits she didn't know much about cricket back then, but that soon changed. There was plenty of time to get acquainted with the game while she was helping to do the teas for the men. Over the years, she got more involved with the off-field side of things. Dad's still proud of the fact that she scored a game at Lakenham, the Norfolk County ground at the time.

After they married, Dad completed his fourth-year Honours while Mum supported them both by working at the Marks & Spencer department stores. Dad got his first teaching job back at his

I like to think it was just like in the movies – a mob of crying babies, a nervous couple with their faces pressed up against the window ... Suddenly they point, 'We'll have that one!'

old grammar school in Norfolk, and Mum found a teaching post as well. All was looking rosy for the young couple.

I was born on 9 June 1975 in Birmingham, England, and was placed for adoption pretty well from birth. I have some West Indian heritage but that's all I know of that particular part of my family tree. Ask me about the branches that have grown since and I'm your man – with a bit of help from the folks about the finer details of course.

I was cared for by a foster mother for a few months before Ken and Barbara Symonds came along. The official story is that they saw a photo of me and then took me for a trial 'outing', but I prefer my version of events (which I trot out for the boys from time to time). I probably spread it on a bit thick, but I like to think it was just like in the movies – a mob of crying babies, swaddled in white in cots behind the nursery glass; a nervous couple with their faces pressed up against the window, scanning the rows of wailing infants ... Suddenly they stop, point and mouth, 'We'll have that one!' I've also been known to add that they only took me on the condition that they could return me if I cried too much, but of course I was a dream from the outset. Great story ... and Mum actually reckons there's a grain of truth to it. I did cry, for most of that first 'test' day it turns out, but as far as she and Dad were concerned, it was one Test that I passed with flying colours. Boom boom.

Watering the garden in Geelong, aged three.

As far as I know, I was nameless until this point. I don't have a middle name, and this is something people assume is because I was adopted, but in reality it was Mum's idea – she doesn't have one and doesn't see the relevance of them and so, as a result, none of us has one. It's just Andrew, Nicholas and Louise Symonds – easy to sign and easy to remember.

Before the deal was sealed, though, the adoption agency needed to be certain that the prospective parents and the baby would bond. It was really for the parents more than anything – if they didn't physically like the look of the kid or just didn't feel at one with it, it gave everyone a chance to step back and start again. I'd say I've got through the trial period – Mum can't take me back now and swap me for a better behaved one.

It might seem odd to be cracking jokes about my situation, and I do realise that for me to end up with a couple like Mum and Dad would have involved plenty of pain and sadness along the way but, with medical science these days giving childless or infertile couples a helping hand, it's easy to forget that thirty-odd years ago, the options were far fewer for a pair of married schoolteachers – he in his late 20s and she in her mid-20s – who were frustrated with their attempts to start a family. It was pre-IVF (which was actually pioneered in Britain) and Mum and Dad would have faced a lengthy spell on a waiting list with the National Health if they wanted to access any of the fertility treatments. They wrestled with the adoption issue, only to find out that there were more people wanting to adopt than there were children available. But then one agency raised the idea of adopting a mixed-race baby.

In doing this book, Mum and Dad told me how hard it was for mixed-race babies born at that time in England. I'm not shocking anyone when I say that this isn't my area of expertise – as any of my mates would no doubt be saying to themselves by now (assuming they haven't skipped this chapter and gone straight to the Cardiff one). But reliable sources have it that back in the 1960s Birmingham was one of England's industrial and manufacturing powerhouses and was always welcoming new workers. As a consequence, the city had a large West Indian immigrant population.

Anyway, Mum and Dad were asked if they'd consider a mixed-race baby and they replied that they'd need a bit of time to think about it. This was just the answer the agency was looking for – too quick a response might have indicated the couple hadn't really thought through all of the implications. Of course, I'm forever grateful: if they'd said 'yes' or 'no' straightaway, it's unlikely I'd be here today. Interestingly, a few experiences in their past had in a sense sowed the seeds for my arrival. At teachers' college they'd done a joint research study on educating West Indian immigrants and integrating them into the English education system. Mum was from Birmingham (a 'Brummie') and had grown up with the influx of migrants into the area, and Dad had played cricket with plenty of West Indians. His dad Wally worshipped the great West Indian cricket trio, the three 'W's – Sir Everton Weekes, Sir Clyde Walcott and Sir Frank Worrell. So, although it was still a leap of faith, they were quietly confident an Anglo–West Indian boy or girl would be a good fit with them.

Once they'd decided, and all the necessary checks had been done, it was a rapid process: from the photo arriving to me going home to a hastily kitted-out nursery was a matter of only a few weeks. I'm told I was a good sleeper once settled, a trait that I've maintained throughout my life, and, apart from Mum having some anxious moments when the adoption agency did its routine follow-up checks, worrying about how tidy the house was and whether everything was being done the right way, we soon got on with becoming a family.

■◀▮▮▶■

I spent my first 18 months in England and was christened there. Not many people know that I've got a French godfather, Bertrand Hullot, but the French connection, if I can use the phrase, recurs a fair bit throughout our lives. My one and only academic prize (and there'll be some out there who are picking up this book again after momentarily dropping it in shock) was for French. It was an Alliance Française award and I got it for reciting a poem. Louise studied French as part of her teaching degree and Dad studied in Paris for a while and has taught French nearly all of his working life. And, of course, I've played my share of French cuts along the way!

As soon as I could walk I was into sport and wouldn't have been much older than twelve months when I got my first bat and ball. They were made of foam, and so my earliest cricketing moments were spent if not on the green playing fields of England, then certainly on the carpets. But the bat and ball weren't my only

The 1988 Alliance Française award winners.

obsessions – apparently I took a shine one day to a navy blue handkerchief. I used to carry it everywhere, and would go on the warpath if it was ever taken off me. Mum ended up getting four or five so she could sneak them off for a wash.

We could have made our lives in England but Dad had his sights set further afield. My grandfather, Wally, had longed to travel and his son had inherited his itchy feet. As a trainee teacher, Dad had had a number of friends who'd left the UK to teach in far-flung places like Kenya, Rhodesia, Canada and Australia. His favourite book as a kid was *The Coral Island* by RM Ballantyne and he had long dreamed of going to the tropics. Mum loved the outdoors too, but wasn't quite as keen to leave her home. Raising her first child (and enjoying the fuss of her family) was a strong grounding factor, but she didn't mind Dad looking, and over time they narrowed down their preferences – at least on paper – to Australia or New Zealand. Canada had been a contender, but they weren't a strong cricketing country and that counted against it as far as Ken Symonds was concerned.

Trout fishing in the Grampians, aged four.

Dad had become mates with a few Aussies at his school and at the cricket club, and slowly started to convince Mum that 'the lucky country' was the place to be. He'd regularly swing by Australia House and bring home pictures and information: one day he showed Mum a photo of the beautiful Blue Mountains, west of Sydney. It must have done the trick: she told him that she could picture herself there, exploring the countryside in her four-wheel drive!

Dad got busy and wrote to independent schools and agencies in Queensland, Victoria, Western Australia and New Zealand. The most promising response came from Geelong Grammar School, which had quite a reputation in England due to the attendance for a time of a certain Prince Charles. They were keen on hiring a French and physical education teacher and their offer arrived by telegram on Christmas Eve in 1976. The job was confirmed on Boxing Day so it was action stations from there: the Symonds family was on the move.

In just under a week we were at the airport ready to go. My first long-haul flight wasn't a bad experience for me, but it was a little uncomfortable for Mum and Dad, who had wet legs for 28 hours due to the under-performance of my new-fangled disposable nappies. Fortunately, things picked up. Geelong Grammar had made a house available for us to live in – it was unfurnished and, with our furniture and most of our gear still on a boat somewhere, we camped indoors for those first three months. Thankfully the school families chipped in with a few bits and pieces, and we did have some cutlery, thanks to Mum lugging it on the plane in her hand luggage. Just try to get away with that these days!

I'm told I was fascinated by the sights and sounds of my new home, especially having access to a yard with a nectarine tree and a chook pen with a couple of chickens. We acclimatised pretty quickly and by the time I was two, we were regularly off camping in the bush as Mum and Dad explored the countryside. Geelong Grammar's campus at Timbertop in the Victorian Alps was a good place to start: it was there that I began to learn something about mountain-stream trout fishing, using spinners, with our friends the Weigalls. Their boys, Phillip, Derek and Mark, were a little older than I was (I would have been around three), but I stuck to them as closely as the leeches in the creeks, learning whatever I could. The Weigall boys have been involved with fishing ever since: Phillip writes books on the subject he and Mark run Millbrook Lakes, a fly-fishing resort in Victoria.

From that early age I was, ahem, hooked, and although I started with trout, and still enjoy that type of fishing to this day, I soon discovered there was a heap of different fish out there. It was the beginning of nearly 18 years of outstanding bush holidays: terrific times and a near perfect way to grow up.

<hr>

Maybe my parents were more settled, maybe more relaxed, maybe it was the fresh Australian air, but in 1977 they conceived naturally and in 1978 my brother Nick was born in Geelong. In a sense he was just what the doctor ordered. I loved having him around, although I worked out fairly quickly that he had a shorter fuse than me and I'd get a reaction if I teased him. I tried to interest him in cricket (mainly so I'd have someone to play with) but hockey turned out to be his sport of choice. We had miniature hockey sticks and cricket bats so we'd invent games that we could play in the house when it was too cold to go outside. We came up with 'lounge cricket', which was played on your knees with a mini bat, with Christmas decorations bound with sticky-tape to make a seam. They were great because they'd really fly if you got them in the middle. I still get a bit of a smile when I see the baubles go up each December.

Billycarting with Nick in Geelong.

People who know me well wouldn't be shocked to hear that pinning down these early memories isn't the easiest of tasks for me. Luckily, Mum and Dad's numbered photo albums going back to my first appearance in the world more than make up for my faulty memory. I am sure about a few things though: for as long as I can remember the most important things in my life outside my family have been sport, fishing and the Australian bush. Mum and Dad have the photos to prove it. Some of the best times of my life were spent camping in places like the Grampians or Woodgate National Park near Bundaberg; catching Bogong moths to go trout fishing in the sparkling ice-cold streams of Mt Buffalo in the Victorian Alps; or building miniature bark huts out of sticks and driftwood on the beach at Noah's Creek on Cape Tribulation. I guess you could say growing up in the bush is as much a part of me as my woolly hair.

CHAPTER 2

THE NORTH

'Talk about mad dogs and Englishmen!' That was the reaction at Geelong Grammar when Dad accepted a job in Far North Queensland after just two years in Victoria. I suppose leaving a prestigious establishment for a smaller boarding school in the 'deep north' was a bit unusual, but Dad uses words like 'adventure' and 'advancement' whenever we discuss it.

In January 1979 we packed up and shifted to mighty Charters Towers, 135 kilometres inland from Townsville. At one point it had been the largest centre in Queensland outside of Brisbane, but that was during its heyday in the 1800s when goldmining made it a bustling, vibrant boomtown. By the time the Symonds clan rolled in, the distinctive buildings in the main streets were some of the only reminders of its earlier prosperity. In the early 1980s it was mainly cattle country and there were a number of boarding schools in the area that catered for students from the numerous properties and rural communities in the region.

The Symonds family in
February 1986.

Among them was All Souls St Gabriel's, a boarding school founded in 1920. Dad was offered a job as the French master and was also made a boarding house master. While he and Mum had liked Geelong, they both wanted to experience what they regarded as the 'real' Australia. When you're three and half, you don't really care where you end up and I'm sure my first year at Charters Towers was a fun one. But no sooner had we set up house than the moving van was back again at the end of the year and we found ourselves leaving the warmth of the north and heading back to Victoria to another old goldmining boomtown, Ballarat. Mum's brother and his family had emigrated to Australia soon after us and had settled there. Then Mum's father, Tony, came out for a holiday and not long after that took early retirement and decided there'd be worse places to spend his twilight years. Mum was keen to be closer to her family, especially her dad, so when a job came up at Ballarat & Clarendon College, Dad took it.

Once again we did a spell of indoor camping while we waited for our furniture to arrive. I started school and quickly learned the most fun to be had was out in the playground, especially as I'd just got my very first tracksuit. It was black and had stripes on it and I thought it was so cool … even before I knew what cool was.

━━

As you've probably guessed, moving house was becoming a bit of a habit for the Symonds family, and in 1984, after four years in Ballarat, Dad took a job back at All Souls in Charters Towers and off we went again. This time, we stayed for five years. The place suited me well – we were living on campus so there were always heaps of kids around and plenty of stuff happening. I went to the local

Fishing at Mt Buffalo in December 1981.

Catholic school, St Columba, until Year 6, and then to All Souls for Years 7 and 8. It was during our time there that the gods of fertility smiled on the Symonds family yet again, and my sister Louise was born in Townsville. Once she was big enough, she joined her brothers' adventures, and created a few for herself as well. When she was just a toddler, she once pushed her trolley full of blocks some 800 metres across the campus where they found her getting ready to tackle the steps to the swimming pool!

Generally, Charters Towers was a kid-friendly environment: Nick and I used to ride our bikes everywhere, exploring the neighbourhoods and eating the 'chiney apples' that grew on a spiky thorn bush (which also happens to be a noxious weed). The fruit would go from rock-hard green to yellow when ripe and tasted a bit like an apple. You knew about it though if you ate too many unripe ones. We'd also devour the fruit from tamarind trees, which we called 'bush lollies' because if you got a nice one, the sticky middle was like toffee and you could suck on them for a good hour or so.

Despite my adventurous spirit – climbing trees, fishing, bike riding, playing sport and eating poisonous fruit – I somehow managed to get through childhood without any major injuries. I had heaps of hairy moments though. I used to do skids and burnouts on my bike on the way from our house to the main oval, but one year they were trying to grow grass there and had strung up some fencing wire to keep people – that is, kids like me – off it. Anyway, I was that pleased to be out of school and back on my bike, I forgot all about it and came flying straight down the slope and hit the wire at full pace. It got me just across the chest, popped straight up under my chin and threw me into the air. I landed on my tailbone, winded, and lay there for a good five minutes but, apart from a scratch under my chin and a bruised ego, I was fine. A few inches higher and it might have been a different story.

Of course, the hijinks didn't stop there: my mates Duncan and Paul Bullock and I would regularly try to knock down a big paper wasps nest that was in a tree down near the school chapel. We were never strong enough to hit it with rocks so one day I pinched a butter knife from the boarding house dining room and had a lash with that. I hit the nest dead centre … and you could hear the hum as out the wasps came. We took off down the road, as fast as we could, laughing at how we had finally got the nest. And then we stopped. Big mistake. They caught us and had their revenge: we received at least twenty stings each for our trouble. That was the last time we pulled that particular stunt.

My only 'serious' injury occurred one arvo when I was about 11 and playing footy on the main oval. I tore a few ligaments in my knee but at the time didn't think it was that bad, so I rode home and carried on as usual. But the next morning when I woke up in my top bunk, my knee was as swollen as a grapefruit and I couldn't bend it, much less climb down the ladder. What was worse was that it coincided with my first pig-hunting trip.

Bung knee or not, I was determined to go on the hunt which was on a property called Fanning Downs on the Burdekin River not far from Charters Towers. In our little party were Louise's godfather, Kent Harrison, and his kids, Dad, Nick and I. Kent shot a big sow but there was a heap of little squealer piglets under a rubber vine that were fair game. He said that if we could catch one alive, we'd be $20 richer, so we were all on fire getting set to chase them. Anyway, we threw a stick in and out they came, scattering in all directions. Of course I had the dud knee and couldn't move anywhere near as fast as the others, so I'd dive for one and miss and land on these goatshead thorns and bindies.

It was looking pretty bleak for the A Symonds Savings Account when one of the little squealers belted out of the bushes straight towards me. I thought, 'Here we go! I'm a chance for 20 bucks now!' In those days, 20 bucks was like a million dollars. Just imagine how many Redskins it could have bought. Anyway, little piggy throws in a swerve, a jink and spins his wheels in the dirt and I didn't lay a single finger on him. I was dark as mud. With a high-pitched oink, my fortune had disappeared into the scrub.

◄▮▮►

If I had to nominate my favourite spot in the world, Cape Town in South Africa, parts of the West Indies, Sri Lanka, and parts of New

Zealand would definitely be on the shortlist but, if forced to pin one down, I reckon I'd choose the Woodgate National Park near Bundaberg in Queensland. It's truly outstanding: long beaches, dunes, scrub and bush … plenty of places for kids to explore and roam without a worry in the world. While we were living up north, we went camping there most Christmas holidays, going fishing all day, building cubby houses in the scrub, having sand-dune fights. One year there was a huge old log on the beach that must have been tossed up in a cyclone and we made that our base, hiding in the hollows and chasing one another, laughing away the days. Those trips made a big impression on me because it was where I started to learn the things I was keen to know. Dad taught me how to fish and how to tie knots for hooks and string sinkers, how to build and light a camp fire, and even, when I was about 13 and pestering the life out of him, how to drive on the beach when the tide went out. Mum played her part as well, providing the expert filleting of the fish we caught.

Dad handled my demands comfortably and wouldn't let me jump into something if he thought I wasn't ready. I went through a period when I desperately wanted a pocketknife, mainly because Dad carried one, but also because it seemed the most useful thing you could possibly own. I'd argue that I needed a proper one, not one of those toy key-ring jobs you'd get at the Charters Towers Show that always broke. Dad would say, 'No, you're not ready yet, I'll think about it.' Eventually he must have thought I was ready, and when I got it I looked after it like gold. I cut myself a few times, usually when modifying tennis balls to make them swing better in our games of backyard cricket. I'd hack all of the fur off one side, and would inevitably take a piece out of myself. The balls swung all right, but they didn't last long because the rubber was so thin they'd split after a few good whacks.

My little sister Louise was like my shadow on a lot of those Woodgate trips. I'd go fishing for whiting off the beach and she'd come down with her bucket and swim and find yabbies and bait for me. Nick would come too but his patience wasn't quite up to a whole day. He preferred building miniature houses and towns out of driftwood and stuff we found in the bush. He was a big cubby builder too, although at times his creativity would get the upper hand. He always wanted to put another level on and then go 'upstairs' while the structural engineer in me was pointing out that we were only using bark and sticks. I'm not at all surprised that he became an architect.

I'll bet, though, that some of his memories aren't quite as glowing as the ones I've been describing. The time I managed to

Nick, Louise and yours truly in July 1985.

hook him through the leg would be one. It was an accident but we couldn't get the hook out so it meant a trip to the hospital in Bundaberg. On another occasion I got one through his eyelid. The Burdekin River was a popular spot – I caught my first really big fish there, a black bream which is like a mangrove jack – but on this particular day I went to cast just as Nick was walking behind me, and caught him right in the eye. Fortunately it missed his eyeball, and 'Dr' Ken Symonds performed the emergency surgery, extracting it as gently as he could. The hook that is, not the eyeball. Apart from the shock, Nick was fine and I'm pretty sure the scar's healed nicely …

■■■▶

Accidents and practical jokes aside, Charters Towers was where my cricket really started to take off. Dad had been encouraging and coaching me on a regular basis from the age of about six or seven and I was always at him to practise, before school, after school … just about any spare moment really. We were probably in the nets five days a week and I'm sure the neighbours thought he was mad. They probably thought he was forcing me, but it was I who was doing the forcing.

Dad was never a big fan of defensive batting, and so one of the first things we worked on was how to drive. He used to throw a ball on a length and get me to move to it and smack it. That way, I could defend against a ball but I'd also be in a position to hit it, which is what I wanted to do. From there, he showed me to how to play back, but again, it was to play a drive or a cut shot, not just defend.

As I improved, we used to work through the shots, and Dad would simulate game conditions. He'd put little rags in the nets to act as fielders and would draw chalk marks for where my feet should

Although Dad taught me to play aggressive cricket, he always emphasised the fun side of it. When I think back, it was amazing I kept my concentration going for that amount of time — I've honestly got the attention span of a goldfish.

move. We were on concrete wickets but he'd get me to imagine it was turf, and even used to draw marks where I'd have to move if it *was* turf. We'd end each session with some games where Dad would give me a mark out of ten for my shots. If I scored three ten out of tens in a row, we'd call it quits. I was an instinctive learner when it came to physical activity – if someone showed me how to do something, I'd usually be able to pick it up after a few attempts. Although Dad taught me to play aggressive cricket, he always emphasised the fun side of it. When I think back, it was amazing I kept my concentration going for that amount of time – I've honestly got the attention span of a goldfish.

◀▮▶

I started playing in junior competitions when I was about eight. I scored my first hundred when I was at St Columba, (112 not out in a final against Richmond Hill State School), although they changed the rules after that, forcing you to retire at 30, as that was closer to what was being played at club level. I managed another century in Year 8 for All Souls against Mt Carmel College, which was pretty rare apparently.

Dad thought I might be better off playing in a stronger competition and suggested I join an under-10s club in Townsville. Mum took a bit of convincing, firstly because she was worried I was too young, and secondly because it would mean a round trip of some 260 kilometres each weekend, but Dad was certain I'd be better off in Townsville and naturally I was keen as. He got in touch with another teacher named Kerry Emery, who was also a Queensland Country player, and arranged for me to join PYC Wanderers. After a few games, Mum came around, mainly because I was enjoying myself so much and Wanderers was such a well-run club.

Even so, it was a huge sacrifice for them. Every Saturday morning at the crack of dawn we'd pile into our Holden Jackaroo and set off, eating bananas and muesli bars for breakfast and listening to John Williamson or Ian McNamara's 'Australia All Over' radio show on the way down the Flinders Highway. There was no air-conditioning so the trip home at lunchtime was usually a warm one. It was tough on the kangaroo population as well – we cleaned up a number over the years going back and forth, especially when we added in a Sunday trip for rep training and then hockey training in winter for Nick and me.

If I didn't get 30 runs – the score at which you had to retire – it was a massive letdown. I expected it and obviously thought I was good enough to get it every week. There were certain bowlers that you had to be careful of and some strong teams, but even back then I was determined to get my haul. Some kids worked out how to milk the 'retire at 30 rule' by reaching 29 and thumping a four or even a six to get 33 or 35, but being small and skinny I had to rely on timing rather than brute force. And Dad would always say, 'Don't be sucked into that, just get your 30 or 31 or whatever it is and walk off.' I did what I was told – most of the time – but if we had that rule today, I'd be farming the strike and trying to put one over the fence for sure once I got to 29!

The North Queensland Under-12 rep trials were something else. I was only ten and still on the small side so I wore small boys' pads and a little thighpad. Most of the other kids were 11 and had full-size gear. My kit fitted me well so I wasn't complaining, but it was clear I was from the bush and there was a fair bit of giggling when I rocked up. Looks aside, I did okay in the trials and got picked.

My first bat – a Symonds junior with a mini-handle Dad had had specially fitted – was the absolute crown jewels. I didn't like lending it to other kids in case it got damaged so, once they'd admired it, I'd whisk it away. They'd be going, 'Mate, can I borrow your bat?' and I'd be saying, 'Nuh, not today.' I was a bit obsessive, but at that age you've only got the one bat and I couldn't risk anything happening to it. Dad still has it somewhere at home. Once I grew a bit more, I got a bigger Symonds, the Tusker, and it was a beauty as well, and then when I was about 12 we ordered a Gray Nicholls single scoop from the Greg Chappell Cricket Centre in Brisbane. I was red-hot to use it but I knew it had to be properly knocked in first. I'm sure I drove Mum mad oiling it, sanding it and whacking it in with a wooden mallet. I finally got the nod from Dad but – and it pains me to say this because they're my current bat sponsor and I'm spoiled rotten with equipment these days – it was the biggest plank ever. I think I only used it twice. It was that tinny I made Dad try it and even he agreed. It went into a school kitbag and I ended up getting a Duncan Fearnley – the Allan Border Five Star – which I used for the rest of my junior days before I landed my first deal with Slazenger when I was 17.

Dad's habit of boundary walking whenever I was batting began in Townsville. He'd roam around the ground so he could watch me

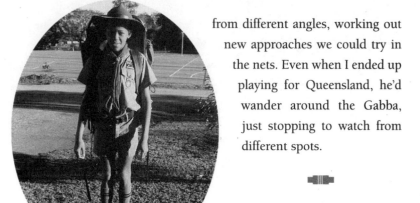

from different angles, working out new approaches we could try in the nets. Even when I ended up playing for Queensland, he'd wander around the Gabba, just stopping to watch from different spots.

A proud scout in 1987.

Although cricket was becoming my number one passion, Mum and Dad insisted I keep up with my bookwork as well, as you'd expect from a pair of teachers. Mum even wanted me to learn a musical instrument, but instead of something cool like the guitar – which might've come in handy in later years around the campfire – I was signed up to learn the flute. I protested long and loud and they eventually relented and switched me to another instrument: the clarinet. Dad reckons that I would have been good at either because I was dextrous enough – more Dexter Poindexter if you ask me. Nevertheless, on Sunday arvos, when all the boarders were getting ready for footy training, I'd be locked in my room, practising. Can you imagine? I'm stuck with this clarinet, almost smelling the Dencorub and gazing out the window at the other kids kicking the footies, the footies I should have been collecting in my cherished role as ball boy and sand boy. Mum wasn't having any of it though: 'Until I hear an hour of something – it can be an hour of *noise* – you're not coming out!'

I shouldn't be too tough on Mum and Dad for trying. I could be stubborn if I didn't want to do something, but they were used to dealing with kids' moods and usually got me to go where they wanted in the end. And let's face it, I had it good. Mum was a home economics teacher so dinnertime was a bonanza, with my skinny legs proving remarkably hollow. I was a bit of a 'fang' man, and loved her moussaka and roast pork and roast chicken with homemade gravy. I wasn't bad on my vegies but every now and then the old brussels sprouts would turn up … I can still hear Mum saying, 'They're full of iron, Andrew, and they're good for you, so please eat them.' I'd tuck into a bit more meat and potato, vainly thinking I could wear the sprouts out by pushing them around the plate.

One night, after batting them from side to side, hoping they'd somehow disappear, I gave up and refused point-blank to go any further.

'They'll be there in the morning,' Mum said.

I thought, 'Oh yeah, right.'

Sure enough, next morning at the breakfast table, there they were, cold and congealed, and you can bet she made certain I didn't leave the table until I had eaten every last one …

Now I know Mum will dispute this story because she reckons she never forced me to eat anything, but I swear it's true: you never forget an encounter like that with brussels sprouts.

And I've avoided them like the plague ever since.

MAKE UP YOUR MIND!

By Adam Dale

One night the Bulls were getting ready to go out after a game. I think we were heading over to someone's place for a barbecue. Anyway, Joey Dawes was taking drink orders and planned to pop into a bottle shop on the way. I asked him to get me half a dozen beers. Joey got a few more orders and then double-checked them. He asked me again how many I wanted and I replied, 'Just six.'

Then Roy leapt in. 'Hang on, Chippin – he's doing you a favour. You just said you wanted half a dozen so make up your mind!'

Adam says: 'I love the fact that Roy was looking out for his mate Joey in this story but didn't miss the chance to have a go at me as well! In all honesty, he's been a good mate over the years and is always ready to lend a hand. He spent two days helping me to build a fence once, and was terrific with our three little girls when they were growing up.'

CHAPTER 3

THE GREAT OUTDOORS

Between the ages of about ten and 15, I played cricket in the State junior championships, and Far North Queensland (FNQ), which revolved around Cairns, was the toughest team to beat. I first came up against Mahbo in the Under-12s when I was in the North Queensland (NQ) team. The old Cairns–Townsville rivalry was alive and well, but we were united in our dislike of the Brisbane teams. We thought they were spoiled and cocky – they had all the flash gear and went to the best schools. It was the standard city–country divide, mixed in with a bit of the old North Queensland suspicion of the big smoke down south.

I may be biased, but back then the best talent came from the bush: Kurt Beale and Troy Gosper from FNQ; Anthony 'Chook' Fowler from Ipswich, who later played first-grade Rugby League for the Gold Coast Seagulls; South East Queenslander Adam Crawford, who's now a professional golfer; my fellow Queensland and

Fishing at Woodgate in 1990.

Australian player Martin Love, who was in the Wide Bay team and a dominant batsman even then; Matthew Mott from South East Queensland; and NQ players Stuart Hodges and Peter Burge, the latter of whom has represented Australia at triple jump and long jump at the Commonwealth and Olympic Games. Wendell Sailor reckons he played against me when he was representing Central Queensland and I still occasionally bump into people who tell me they got me out in those carnivals. I just tell them I don't remember when I get out!

In 1989 we moved down to the Gold Coast. Leaving Charters Towers was tough: for a young family, it had been idyllic, but Dad, ever conscious of my budding career, knew that Brisbane was where the action was. There was also the consideration of university for Nick and Louise, although not for me …

All Saints Anglican School had just opened at Mudgeeraba, a peaceful little town on the Gold Coast hinterland, and Dad was appointed Head of Senior School and Assistant to the Headmaster. I'd been in Year 8 in Charters Towers but I repeated the year at All Saints when I started, mainly because being a new school, it wasn't offering Year 9. When I'd started school in Ballarat, I went up from Prep to Grade 1, so I'd always been a bit younger than most of the other kids. Academically, repeating a year was probably a good thing.

The Gold Coast was a major culture shock. There'd be a casual day and it was like a fashion parade. Up north we'd run around in mismatched stubbies or footy shorts and whatever T-shirt you'd pull out of the top drawer, but down on the Coast, the kids had the latest boardies and coordinated T-shirts. They went surfing every day and

Wanderers Player of the Year 1986/87.

were living the Coast lifestyle and I certainly felt – and looked – way out of place. I was also shy in those days, and would stand back and work out what was going on before leaping in. Soon after we arrived, we went hiking on a school camp near Wolffdene in the Albert River valley. As you do, I caught us some yabbies in one of the waterholes and stowed them in my water bottle to keep them alive until we got to camp and could cook them up. Well, you should have seen the reactions from the other kids when I pulled them out: you'd swear I'd come from another planet!

■◀||▶■

I started playing junior cricket at Palm Beach–Currumbin in the Under-15s in 1989 where I hooked up again with Matthew Mott, who I'd played against in Dalby in the State titles earlier in the season.

Motty was a hard-hitting, quick-witted left-hander who had a seemingly photographic memory for any mistakes or mishaps that might befall you. I went to the State titles with the South East Queensland team later that season, and made the Queensland Under-15 team. But Motty recalled a conversation he'd had before the titles with our club coach, a top bloke by the name of Les Ferguson, about my selection chances. Les was a bit doubtful and reckoned that while I was a good batsman, I could cost a team ten to 15 runs in the field. Now I *was* a bit lazy in those days and his comments were probably well justified, but whenever Motty bumps into Les the first thing he says is, 'How about that Roy, hasn't he come a long way?'

I liked playing on the Coast even though the junior competitions weren't as consistently strong as they were in Townsville, mostly because every summer the kids would be lured away by the surf. You'd be fine up until the Christmas holidays and then after that, your teams would be down to eight and nine players. I was never really attracted to the surfing lifestyle, even though I had a boogie board and loved the water; I preferred to fish off a surf beach than go wading through the shore break.

In 1990 the local Gold Coast competition existed in its own right, separate from the main club cricket premiership in Brisbane. It was the same story with Beenleigh and Logan City. You'd play juniors and then go into the seniors, where you'd play other teams from your area. Queensland Cricket had identified that the corridor between Brisbane and the Gold Coast was booming and proposed the XXXX Premiership be expanded. So the Gold Coast Dolphins were invited into the 1990/91 Brisbane premiership and, as a part of their admission, were also asked to field a team in the Under-19 competition. It was perfect for young fellas like Motty and me and other promising players from the area like Jeff Pfaff, Scott Muller, Trevor Greentree, Paul Spence and Brett Crichton, because we were able to play at a higher level than was possible on the Coast, without having to move to Brisbane and sign up with one of the existing clubs.

I was 16 when I started playing Under-18s and 19s and I used to jump out of bed like a kid on Christmas Day whenever there was a Dolphins training session. Being able to mix with current and former Test players like Dirk Wellham, Greg Campbell and Craig McDermott, and ex-Queensland players like Steve Storey and wicketkeeper Peter Anderson, was priceless. It did get exciting in the nets sometimes, with a tearaway Scott Muller proving a handful for the younger blokes. There was a promising batsman from Mackay, a council road-worker by the name of Terry Oliver, who was a good scout and made a strong impression on me. Who'd have thought 15 years later he'd *still* be trying to teach me how to bat!

I really wouldn't have got where I am today without the Dolphins. Having exposure to those experienced players was a godsend, and they gave me an insight into what cricket was all about at a senior level. It was a bit like when I was a little fella who wanted to be around the big kids at boarding school: you looked up to them and you learned from them. The following season in 1991/92 saw me gain more exposure, playing my share of second grade on the Saturday, and then fronting up for the Under-19s on the Sunday.

Because we were a new club, there were opportunities to make rapid advancement and I made my first-grade debut as a 17-year-old that summer for the last one-day game of the season against Sandgate-Redcliffe. It was challenging, but I got a few runs so at least felt it wasn't completely beyond me. Even then I was a bit of a headstrong batsman and would take on some impossible challenges, which prompted one of my team-mates, Brett Crichton, to dub me 'SAO' – or Six And Out. Queensland Youth team coaches Jimmy Hunter and Ashleigh 'Toot' Byron would say that when a ball was bowled at me, I'd have three or four shots in mind and would inevitably choose the riskiest one. When it came off, you looked a genius but when it didn't, there was the inevitable head-shaking from all involved.

The 1991/92 season was a strong one for Queensland in the Under-17 and Under-19 carnivals and I think the successes paved the way for the bonanza post-1995. Motty was playing in the Under-19s and scored 222 not out while I managed 204 against South Australia for the Under-17s. Kevin Curyer, a fast bowler from Laidley whose initials KC earned him the nickname of 'Sunshine', won the bowler of the tournament award, and he and I were named in the Australian Under-17 squad, a selection which earned us both a week at the Cricket Academy in Adelaide. In addition, Motty, Jimmy Maher and Martin Love were selected in the Australian Under-19 squad.

I learned a lot about cricket, and about life in general, during those early seasons with the Dolphins. The first-grade team would bus it to the away games – a great bonding exercise – and on the way home, if we were lucky, the older blokes would let the younger ones have a beer or two. I wasn't that keen on the amber nectar at the time – which I know may surprise a few people now – so the best way to get through one, and not get the older blokes off-side, was to tip it into the chocolate thickshake I'd buy when we stopped at McDonald's or Hungry Jacks. Of course, Mum and Dad were usually in the car following us, and were probably suspicious as to why I had to order four thickshakes …

◄▮▮►

Motty and I both earned first-grade starts with the Dolphins early in the 1992/93 season, and again backed it up by playing Under-19s on Sunday. Opening the innings against South Brisbane in a one-day game at Boundary Street, which was actually Wynnum-Manly's home ground, we put on 446 before retiring. Motty whacked 208 not out, with 20 fours and four sixes, while I hit 220 not out, with 27 fours and 14

With Matthew Mott and our scores.

sixes. It was a tough day for the Souths bowlers as we were both coming off hundreds the previous Sunday when we'd put on 201 for the first wicket and had our eye in from the outset on a lightning-quick ground and perfect batting strip. Our coach Bill Pippen, a great club man who had worked tirelessly during the early years of the Dolphins, was torn between seeing us do something spectacular and deciding that enough was enough. He came out at drinks after 36 overs and suggested we head in to give the other blokes a go. Motty was captain and thought that was fair enough but I was young and impetuous and had the bit between my teeth. 'Boys, what if we both retire and we lose some quick wickets and then find ourselves in trouble?' I argued.

Motty and Billy gently pointed out that we were already 0-446. It was a fair cop and so off I went. The next bloke in, Jason Mills, hit 85 off as many balls and we ended up posting 3-585 from 50 overs. Apparently that score is the highest in a limited overs game in minor cricket, which includes everything except 'List A' matches (One Day Internationals and National domestic one-day competitions).

That season I scored my debut first-grade century against Wynnum-Manly at Kerrydale, and was selected in the Queensland Colts team for its southern tour to Sydney, Melbourne and Canberra. I was picked as 12th man for the annual Syd Gregory Cup match between Queensland and New South Wales at Hurstville Oval, and witnessed first-hand the power of a young lefthander from Lismore by the name of Adam Gilchrist. Gilly and Jason Arnberger, who later played for Victoria, smashed centuries against us. I also got to play against the ACT at Manuka Oval, where the scorecard records that one G Gregan was caught by A Symonds off the bowling of Mark Shackel for 18. George was batting at number eight and was an enthusiastic fieldsman and frequent appealer from the covers. Some might say that the skills learned in those games stood him in good stead for his future role as captain of the Wallabys Rugby Union side. On reflection, the things I learned on my first Colts tour, and the Youth teams and the Gold Coast Dolphins, stood me in good stead too.

Playing for the Queensland Under-17s
in Canberra in 1992.

JUST HIT IT
By Adam Dale

After training one day with Roy, Andy Bichel, Ian Healy, Jimmy Maher, Michael Kasprowicz, Wade Seccombe and yours truly, Roy asked Bic why he'd written the letters 'T' and 'P' on the shoulders of his bat. Bic said it was to remind himself of the importance of 'Time' and 'Patience' when he was out in the middle.

Wade then asked Roy what he'd put on the back of his bat and he replied 'S' and 'W'. We were all intrigued and immediately asked him what that stood for.

'Swing hard,' he said, and looked puzzled when we all fell about laughing.

Adam says: 'Once Roy realised what he'd said, he laughed as hard as the rest of us. I reckon Chuck [Wade Seccombe] set him up because he took the odds to it that there would be something quotable. As it turns out, it's become part of the team shorthand whenever Roy bats: "Hey Roy, looks like it's time for a bit of SW now."'

CHAPTER FOUR

WHY 'ROY'?

'**W**hy "Roy"?' is something I've been asked more times than 'Why did you play *that* shot?' In truth, there's no easy answer to either question; the only certainties are that I've had the nickname since my teens and that coaching and coaches are at least partly responsible (for both). Of course, there have been plenty of 'Roy' theories over the years: as a kid I liked kicking a soccer ball around and some say that I earned the name after the English cartoon-strip hero 'Roy of the Rovers'. Mum and Dad are not so sure. Another is that I got the name due to some resemblance to the Brisbane Bullets basketball star Leroy Loggins, an American import who was a dominant force in the NBL during the 1980s and '90s. Hmm, maybe. One Adelaide fan thought Roy must have come from the French word for king – 'roi' – which is pretty flattering though wrong, because as far as I'm concerned (and apologies to any Elvis fans) there's only one king and that's Wally Lewis, the Queensland and Australian Rugby League legend.

Ready for the Australian Under-19s
tour of India in 1994.

I like being called 'Roy'. It fits on a number plate for starters, it's easy to call out in the field, and, well, it sort of suits me.

I tend to think two of my youth coaches at Queensland Cricket, Toot Byron and Jim Hunter, were the true instigators and yes, Leroy Loggins was partly behind it. After school, Mum would drive me to training for the Queensland Cricket Emerging Players squad at the Gabba. Being a shy 14-year-old, fresh from the bush, I wasn't exactly responsive to Toot and Jimmy's suggestions and no doubt came over as having typical teenage 'attitude'. Anyway, each week Toot would drive past a petrol station on the way to the Gabba where the great Leroy Loggins worked. Discussing my progress one day, Toot remarked to Jimmy, 'Does this kid think he's as cool as Leroy Loggins or something?' Jimmy picked up on it and the next week called me 'Leroy' which ended up as 'Roy' or 'Royston'. It didn't really bother me one way or the other; I would have been just as happy with 'Symmo'.

Later, when my then-girlfriend Brooke Marshall and I got a Labrador pup, for some reason we called him 'Roy' as well. There were occasional moments of confusion when one of the Roys was in strife for something; you'd hear 'Roy!' being shouted and spin around to see the dog being roused on. I like being called 'Roy' though. It fits on a number plate for starters, it's easy to call out in the field, and, well, it sort of suits me.

◼◩▮▶

I think good coaches are vital to any cricket player's development and I've been lucky enough to have been taught by some of the very best. Dad was the first and got the ball rolling when I was a nipper; in Townsville I came under the tutelage of Bill Pacey, Kerry Emery, Stan Huen, and Eric Adams, who now works for Queensland Cricket and is still a good sounding board for me and Mahbo; while down south, Jim Hunter, the late Peter 'Sting' Charles and of course Toot all introduced something more to my game.

Toot is a former high school English teacher and has been an influential cricket and rugby union coach for many years. He's highly intelligent and a real character, and gets a kick out of challenging his players. He coached me when I was selected for the Queensland Colts team as a 17-year-old and in subsequent games. Peter Charles, a former fast bowler for Norths in Brisbane, was a bit like Toot – a great teacher and a great communicator who would stretch you whenever he could. Jimmy Hunter was a talented cricketer who'd been in the State squad and represented the Queensland Colts before moving into coaching. He was very strong on the biomechanical side of things and later became John 'Buck' Buchanan's assistant at the Queensland Bulls. He and his brother Richard created the 'Canalyst' or Cricket Analyst computer system which Buck introduced with such success, prompting the rapid growth of computer-based capture and analysis systems. Jimmy coached me at Queensland Under-17 level in 1991 when I scored 204 during the National titles in Canberra. He had this great way of explaining complex biomechanical observations simply, which suited me. He used to talk about 'cracking the whip', which was basically a way of reminding bowlers to lock up their delivery stride and front arm at the point of delivery so that all the energy, and therefore the ball, was released at maximum velocity. He loved my bat speed and the fact I used a lighter bat than a lot of players my age, which fell in with his theory that you were better off swinging a lighter bat faster than using a heavy bat which couldn't be swung as fast. He was outstanding at hitting catches for us when we were working on our fielding – he would always manage to put the ball so you had to stretch or lunge for it. My fielding really began to improve during those sessions.

After Toot and Jimmy, I had the good fortune to learn from former NSW and Australian fast bowler Dave Gilbert. Dave was the inaugural Queensland Academy of Sport coach, and took us on an eye-opening tour of South Africa in 1993. He was a laidback bloke but he ran a tight ship and was the forerunner of what I was to encounter at first-class level.

When I first made it into Queensland Sheffield Shield squad training, the legendary Jeff Thomson was in charge, and you can imagine what it was like rubbing shoulders with a bloke who had been such a larger-than-life player when you were a kid. Thommo was an old school coach, almost like one of the players at times, but he read and understood the game beautifully. The youngsters like myself, Matthew Mott and Shawn Flegler kept our heads down to avoid being called a 'reptile' or worse, which wasn't easy given we were that excited to be hanging with guys like Thommo and Australian players like Allan Border, Craig McDermott and Ian Healy.

I was lucky enough to attend the Australian Cricket Academy under Rod Marsh in Adelaide in 1994. Rod's attitude was that if you did the work and practised hard, you could do whatever you put your mind to. He was tough but fair, as I guess he had to be with more than a dozen young blokes brimming with energy and mischief and, like myself, living away from home for the very first time. I managed to keep out of strife most of the time, although I was banned for driving for a month after being caught thrashing the team bus ... while not wearing my P plates. Not much got past Rod and he kept an eye on us via a monthly interview, before which we'd have various tests, including getting our skin-folds done, to ensure we weren't burning the candle at both ends. It didn't matter though: during one of these meetings Rod famously uttered to one scholar, 'Son, your skin-folds just keep coming down. Are you drinking too much piss to eat?'

Returning to Queensland later that year, I entered the world of Professor Von Slickstein, aka John 'Buck' Buchanan. Buck was like a cartoon mad scientist in those early days and on occasion, I half expected him to turn to us and say, 'Now pay attention because this really *is* rocket science.' He'd talk about where the ball should be

Nursing a broken foot in Geelong in January 1994.

landing and where it had been hit and how we could stop runs and score runs, and then would pump all the information into a computer. At the end of a Shield game he'd present us with a pile of printouts but I told him straight up I wasn't going to read them. He said: 'That's fine, just throw them in the bin. If it's not for you, it's not for you.'

I got to know Buck when he was with the Bulls, and have since forged a strong relationship with him during his run with the Australian team. I admire the way he thinks outside the square and finds ways to challenge us, even if some of it still goes miles over my head. On the way to the 2001 Ashes tour, he bought everyone copies of a book called *Who Moved My Cheese?* by the American author Spencer Johnson. Well, I'd love to know who-dunnit because I never actually finished it! But that's Buck, he genuinely cares and is interested in all aspects of our development. Even our futures. He thinks I should network harder and keep an eye out for something concrete for when the cricket's over. He's right. Maybe there's a bait and tackle shop out there waiting for a new owner …

Whether you get him or not, Buck has fundamentally changed the game and everyone since has had to copy him. But that's not to say *everything* he advocates makes sense. During my contract talks with Cricket Australia in 2006, I was getting a little passionate about where I stood in regards to Test cricket and wanting to nail down a spot. As I drew breath, Buck suggested that if I was really serious, then perhaps I should step down from one form of the game – one-day cricket – and devote myself to the Test arena. David Boon was at the talks and I could see his chin almost hit the table. I asked Buck why in the world I would give up something I was getting the hang of for something there was no guarantee I'd get a go at anyway.

Buck just said softly, 'Royster, it was merely a suggestion.'

At this Boonie couldn't contain himself. 'I'm f***ing glad it was only a suggestion!'

But that's Buck (and Boonie) – never afraid to voice a radical idea if he thinks it might be useful to the process.

His departure from Queensland brought Bennett King onto the scene. Kingy had a ferocious work ethic and a sharp eye for technical flaws and improvements in a player. He quickly worked out what made me tick and would do things like send me out of the nets and tell me to go and hit balls on the bowling machine if he felt that's what I needed. He came from a different background – first-grade Rugby League in New South Wales – but was able to slot into the system that Buck had set up and make it his own. The ex-Leaguey used to come out a bit sometimes, especially in some of the games of touch football, but we enjoyed a great run of success under him, winning a hat-trick of Pura Cup titles. He went onto the Cricket Academy for a while before taking over as the West Indies coach.

Terry 'Tess' Oliver followed Kingy and over the past few years has been generous with his time and advice, particularly making sure I'm not too distracted outside of the game. He's sharp in picking up on when I've got the dirts, but is a great one for making us think of other people and how our actions affect them. We've got a strong connection, in part I think because he came down from Mackay to play first-grade cricket with the Dolphins when they first started in the Brisbane competition and was one of the players I looked up to when I was playing in the Under-18s and 19s. I was thrilled for him when the Bulls won the Pura Cup in 2005/06 because he'd put his heart and soul into the team and had helped get us to a number of finals without luck until then.

SALE OF THE CENTURY

By Jimmy Maher

Back when he was in his 20s, Roy was looking through a real estate magazine that featured rural properties. He came across one that he was quite keen on – it had a homestead, a creek, dams and so on – and the price was around $250,000. We talked about it for a while and then Roy confidently stated that he could get it for $260,000.

I couldn't disagree with him. 'Roy,' I said, 'I'm sure you'd get it for that price.'

His reasoning was that if he really wanted it, he was sure to get it by offering more.

Jimmy says: 'After this exchange, there followed a fairly lengthy discussion about the "dos" and "don'ts" of buying property. You can excuse Roy for being a little naïve in this instance but it just showed that if he wants something badly enough, he will go the extra yards to get it.'

CHAPTER 5

RUNNING WITH THE BULLS

My last year at All Saints in 1993 promised all those outstanding teenage milestones: cars, girls and finally finishing school. But I also had to work in a cricket tour of South Africa in September with the Queensland Academy of Sport, as well as a big summer of training with the Queensland Sheffield Shield squad. It's probably no surprise that the schoolwork took a back seat. There were three of us in that final year who didn't sit for the Queensland Core Skills Test and so didn't get an OP (Overall Position), which would have enabled us to go on to tertiary studies. One went on to become a boilermaker and the other was Steven Laurence who played AFL for the Brisbane Lions and St Kilda.

I'm often asked what I would have become if it hadn't been for cricket. I'd not done any part-time work as a teenager, mainly due to my sporting commitments, but I was confident enough (and thought I had the necessary skills) that I could have found a trade if I'd had to. Dad and I had mucked about building things when I was a kid and I expect I would have looked at getting an apprenticeship with a builder or doing some sort of TAFE course. I always fancied myself with a tool belt on, although the workload would have taken a bit of getting used to. I thank my lucky stars things worked out as they did. I look back now and realise that cricketers of my generation have had it better than any previous generation in a lot of ways, with the lucky ones not having to hold down a regular job outside the game. I know it wasn't always like this.

My first car was a red Subaru wagon and it was an absolute rocket. We picked it up from a teacher friend of Dad's by the name of Jeremy Roberts, the very same bloke in fact who'd sold me my first bat back

With Brooke and our dog (also called Roy!).

in Ballarat. I also started going out with this gorgeous blonde from Year 11. I'd known Brooke Marshall since I started at the school and we'd been friendly before things got more serious. She used to do speech and drama and was into dancing and had this great smile which, for a young bloke, was irresistible. I wouldn't say I was love-struck at first, but I did spend a lot of time just grinning when I was around her. We had a lot of fun in my last year and I had my first bout of homesickness when I had to go on tour in September.

It was the first time the Queensland team had been to South Africa and we had a handy line-up, including Martin Love and Andy Bichel, who had both played first-class by then, and Jimmy Maher and Matthew Mott. There were also players like Scott Williams and Jeff Thomas, and Andrew Bailey, a talented opener who finished up our leading batsman on the tour with more than 400 runs at an average of 100 plus. The side was coached by Dave Gilbert and managed by Trevor Hohns, not that long retired from playing for Queensland and Australia. We had a win, a loss and a draw and while I didn't get the runs I would have liked, I wouldn't have swapped a single moment.

The tour over, it was back to the books and the demands of the 1993/94 summer, starting with the Dolphins and also the Queensland Colts and Under-19 teams. At some point during that period, I developed a niggling pain in my foot – nothing serious, I thought – but annoying nonetheless. One dewy morning during warm-ups for the Queensland Colts team against NSW at St Lucia, I slipped over while fielding a ball, and battled to stand up again. It turned out I'd broken a bone in my foot and it needed a pin. I was on crutches for my graduation, (a good excuse not to dance, actually), and went away as captain of the Queensland Under-19 team still on crutches, missing the first game or two while I was waiting for the bone to heal.

Queensland made the semi-finals that season and I was able to score a century in my first game back, but I battled with the pressures of the captaincy and was secretly relieved to be named in the Australian Under-19 team that was to tour India in March in 1994. But before I could go looking for my passport, there was the small matter of my debut for Queensland. I was a late call-up to play in a one-day Mercantile Mutual Cup game in February 1994 and, after making a mad dash to the airport to get to Adelaide, can report that the day was a forgettable one on a few counts. We were sent in on a greentop and were rolled for just 119, with yours truly adding five before being caught behind by Tim Nielsen off the bowling of Greg Blewett. The South Australians then raced along to 0-120, with me dropping Darren Lehmann at point, and it was all over red rover.

There wasn't time to dwell on it before my bags were packed and I was away again; this time to India. Over the years I've developed a real fondness for the country and its people, but as a teenager coming from a comfortable background, it was both challenging and confronting. We'd heard all the stories about the subcontinent and how hard it was to tour there and that no doubt contributed to how we handled it. Most of us got sick and probably didn't enjoy ourselves as much as we might have. We played three Youth Tests – in Chennai, Mumbai and Thiruvananthapuram (a place I would never send a postcard from unless it was printed on the front because there is no way I could come close to spelling it) – and three Youth One Day Internationals in Vadodara, Ahmedabad and Rajkot. The Australian team was full of future first-class and international stars – Mike Hussey, Brett Lee, Jason Gillespie, Matt Nicholson, Corey Richards,

Rob Baker, Peter Roach, Jerry Cassell and Matthew Anderson – while India's big gun was VVS Laxman, or 'Very, Very Special' as he later became known to Australian teams.

Having played mostly on the well-grassed Brisbane pitches, India's dry, dusty 'bunsen burners' were a bit of an unknown quantity, but I was surprised to find them to my liking. We drew the first Test and lost the second, with Laxman hitting 150 and 77. The Vellyani Agricultural College Ground in Thiruvananthapuram, (yes, I did have to look this up again to be sure of spelling it right) also seemed to suit me, and I managed to knock up 163 in our first innings. We won the third Test to draw the series, with a second innings 95 not out from captain Rob Baker steering us to a six-wicket win. I added 93 and 58 to the tour aggregate while Brett Lee gave notice of what was to come, bowling with rare pace to take four wickets in each innings. India won the ODI series 2-1.

After India it was home to the Gold Coast where I got a part-time job as a groundsman back at All Saints before winging my way to the Cricket Academy in Adelaide for the remainder of the 1994 off-season for another stint under the watchful eye of Rod Marsh. Happily, this time, I didn't need my P plates.

CHAPTER 6

THE MOTHER COUNTRY COMES CALLING

In November 1994, at the age of 18, yet another dream came true: I made my Sheffield Shield debut for Queensland. Under the care of new coach John 'Buck' Buchanan, the team had been rechristened the Bulls the season before, and the team's senior statesman was none other than the mighty Allan Border. In that first season, AB was charged with keeping an eye on me and the two other debutantes, Shawn Fleger and Motty, and although we probably didn't realise it at the time, AB was the right man for the job.

An imposing presence on the field, and one of the fiercest competitors in the game, AB's 'Captain Grumpy' reputation had mellowed over the years and I think he quite enjoyed his newfound domestic responsibilities. The rest of the team used to joke that it was like seeing dad and the kids going out to the game but I suspect AB liked the fact that once we younger blokes got used to him, we relaxed a bit, acted up (from time to time), and certainly didn't put him on a pedestal. Don't get me wrong – we respected him and when we were out on the field we hung off his every word – but it went both ways too. In his last season, AB was having trouble with his form and Motty and I suggested he join us for a few 'Invers' drills (named after John Inverarity). He could easily have told us to get nicked, but was more than happy to give it a go and, coincidentally or not, got some runs in his next innings. He told us that one of his regrets was never having the level of coaching and drills that we'd had as youngsters; when AB was coming through the ranks, it was more a case of fending for yourself. All things considered, I reckon he did okay.

The first game was against NSW at the SCG. I was nervous of course, but walking out onto that hallowed turf felt like the most natural thing in the world. The SCG was a spinners' track in those days and my off-spin sure came in handy. Being an unknown helped too, and I took 3-77 in the first innings, capturing Mark Taylor, Mark Waugh and Michael Bevan – with Wade 'Chuck' Seccombe stumping Taylor and Bevan! Credit should go to Chuck's fast hands, rather than my spinning ability, and I should mention that Junior Waugh was 113 and Bevo was 103, so I wasn't exactly ripping through them. I fell to spin as well in my two bats – bowled for 21 and leg before wicket for nine – both at the hands of the left-arm spinner and NSW policeman Anthony Kershler. We ended up losing the game by ten wickets, not exactly the start you'd hope for, but you've got to expect the occasional bloody nose when you take the training wheels off for the first time.

■◀█▐▶■

The hanky was out the next week as well against Western Australia at the WACA. The Australian Cricket Board was trialling day/night Shield games and while not all the states were set up, Queensland

and WA had both scheduled games that began in the afternoon and finished under the lights. We used an orange ball, then later a yellow one and, for whatever reason, the shine stayed on them longer and when you added dew and floodlights to the equation, batting became a challenge and a half. The balls resembled tracer bullets when you hit them across the turf but they did plenty off the wicket and in the air. I reckon everyone who played one of those games back then should have had ten runs added to their averages.

I only batted once in that second game. After getting away to a brisk start with a few fours and a six, I was skittled for 26 by Big Jo Angel, who had a spring in his step like all the quicks as soon as the lights come on. In the end we were lucky and won by seven wickets. What impressed me most was the 38-year-old AB top-scoring with 73 in his first dig and 54 not out in his second. It was an important lesson for a young player, one of many to come: when things aren't to your liking you've got to try even harder. I guess there's something in the old saying, 'when the going gets tough, the tough get going'.

<hr>

England had been dusted in the first Test of the Ashes at the Gabba in late November 1994, and their next first-class game was against the Bulls in the garden city of Toowoomba. I was playing for the Cricket Academy at the time and didn't expect a call-up, but when AB had to withdraw at the last minute, I found myself smack bang in the middle of seven consecutive (and glorious) days of cricket.

England won the toss, went into bat and quickly rattled up 6-507 with Mike Gatting contributing a double ton and John Crawley a respectable 91. Toowoomba's Heritage Oval is mid-sized and its excellent value batting strip no doubt helped the Poms. But it helped us too and when it was our turn, Stu Law peeled off a handy 91 in the run chase. My old mate Mahbo and I then stepped up and were over the moon to be not out at stumps on day two, what with the likes of Devon Malcolm being fairly lively and Angus Fraser and Phil Tufnell keeping things tight.

 **Whenever I'm feeling under the pump, I tell myself that sometimes we can't always be works of art – we have to settle for just colouring in between the lines.**

At the end of our innings, Mahbo and I had batted for most of the third day, finishing with an unbeaten partnership of 205, helping Queensland to 4-392 declared. Mahbo had scored 100 not out and I'd picked up 108 not out from 127 balls, which made me the youngest player to score a first-class hundred for Queensland. I was 19 years and 195 days old, and like your average 19-year-old, was all over the place when it came to taking notice of things like that. Mahbo would have faced twice as many balls as me and happily describes his work that day as 'scrappy', but while his innings might not have been the prettiest, the fact was he still scored a hundred. There have been days when I might as well have been batting left-handed the way things were going, but I clearly remember his innings that day and whenever I'm feeling under the pump, I tell myself that sometimes we can't always be works of art – we have to settle for just colouring between the lines.

The ensuing media conference was my first taste of things to come. As we got into it, questions were asked about our backgrounds, and when someone revealed that I was been born in England and emigrated here, you could almost hear the buzz among the visiting journos. 'And he's *English*, you say? Dear me, that is interesting. I'll just let the office know ... Do you want to play for England? When were you adopted? Do you ever want to meet your natural mother? Are you *sure* you don't want to play for England?' Poor old Jimmy only got one question and that was what was it like to bat alongside me! It was daunting, no two ways about it, but I did my best and answered them as honestly as I could. I didn't want to play for England, I didn't want to meet my natural mother but I did consider myself an Aussie. And that was that.

In the second innings, England chased some quick runs and declared at 8-236, setting us a target of 351 which Haydos and 'Tank' Barsby took a liking to from the outset. Haydos was a few seasons into his career by then and to see a bloke who was not much older than me play with such determination and maturity was truly inspiring. He made 119 and Tank made 101 as they put on 231 for the opening partnership. Tank was more like me, in that he loved to hit the ball hard, but he also knew when to take the foot off the throttle and gear down. This was a lesson I was going to have to learn a number of times before I was ready to graduate. After the Bulls' promising start, it went downhill quickly and we were dismissed for 314 as Phil Tuffnel spun his way through us to take 5-71. My second innings contribution was a measly seven.

Between Christmas and New Year I got another run with the Bulls when we played Zimbabwe in Maryborough. We won by four wickets, but the left-arm fast bowler David Brain dismissed me for 35 in the first

Adam Dale and I soak up some Scottish sun during the Australia 'A' tour in 1998.

innings, an early instance in my first-class career where Brain outdid brawn ... Haydos underlined his consistency with 64 and 90 not out. I didn't realise it at the time, but I was staring at the inspiration I needed if I was going to go further and be more than just a one-trick pony.

Playing against England that year and fielding all the journos' questions had sparked my curiosity in 'the mother country' and I began giving serious thought to spending a season or two over there. It was a sort of rite of passage for many young and aspiring Aussie cricketers and, depending on how good you were and the amount of interest you attracted, you could get a run as either an amateur or a professional in one of the many League competitions in England or Scotland. The club would normally arrange somewhere for you to live and perhaps some part-time work, while some of the wealthier clubs might even pay you a wage. And because I had been born in England, I had the added advantage of being able to go along without work-permit dramas and the paperwork that usually went with it.

Dad had a few UK contacts but, as it turned out, both Dave Gilbert, the QAS coach, and Ian Healy had already floated my name with the English County side Gloucestershire and the good news was they were keen on bringing me over. A one-year deal was struck just before we played England in Toowoomba and Dad went over the contract for me and made sure I didn't sign anything that might lock me into playing for England. I was excited but torn – the move meant leaving my comfort zone, my family, friends and, of course, Brooke. But it was a once-in-a-lifetime opportunity and so I packed my bags and said my goodbyes.

Upon arriving in Gloucestershire, which is a pretty County in south-western England, I was billeted with a lovely couple, Suzanne and Nick Finch, who are still good family friends. That season I got to rub shoulders with the likes of the England Test wicketkeeper Jack Russell, and their star import, the Indian pace bowler Javagal Srinath. Even though I'd played first-class cricket in Australia and had represented Australia at Under-19 level, being English-born meant that I wasn't considered an import. Their other overseas player was the great West Indian fast bowler Courtney Walsh, who played for them between 1984 and 1998. Between Jack and Courtney, I had two outstanding instructors on the art of cricket and the quirks of life.

I was expecting only to play in the Second XI, but was fortunate to be picked for a practice game against Leicester where I scored 80-odd, thus earning me a spot in the starting side for the first County game of the summer against Surrey at The Oval. Despite the big change in my surroundings, things must have agreed with me because I finished the first day with 161 not out. Knowing Mum and Dad would have been wondering how I had got on, I made an excited call home from a phone box right after it was over; no matter it was in the wee hours of the morning in Australia!

In the end we lost that game, but my performance attracted a bit of media curiosity, something with which I wasn't all that comfortable even though I knew it went with the territory.

I followed up my ton on debut with another hundred against Somerset and was as happy as a fat spider. But no sooner had the gold dust settled than the questions over my eligibility status began. At the start of the season, every player had had to sign the Test and County Cricket Board's registration papers. The document included a new clause stating that you had to play for England if you happened to be selected. Dad and I argued that being an English-born Australian, and possessing an English passport, meant that I should be allowed to play County cricket without having to play for the international side. Matter closed.

Or so we thought.

I decided to knuckle down and concentrate on my cricket, hoping the whole thing would blow over, but when former England Test captain Graham Gooch came out and publicly questioned my motives, it became hard to keep a low profile. Gooch attacked both my eligibility and the system, and while he maintained it wasn't personal, our subsequent on-field meeting put paid to that. For

With Mum and Dad in Gloucestershire.

someone who used to think the only claws I had to worry about were the ones on our dogs, I was learning fast.

Mum and Dad had flown over, courtesy of the club, and almost before he'd had time to unpack, I'd dragged Dad down to the nets for a bit of good old-fashioned father and son bonding. I was feeling out of sorts – in part due to the furore over my eligibility – and my early good form had flagged. Thankfully, Dad knew my game back to front, and after a pep talk and a few specific practice routines, I felt like a new man. It worked a treat because when I fronted up against Essex at Cheltenham I scored a tidy hundred. But then things soured: Graham Gooch happened to be playing for Essex and inevitably we exchanged a few heated words on the field. All part and parcel. But later on, when he was given out, he spat in my direction as he walked off. I let it go – he didn't spit *on* me and I didn't want it to blow up. What happens on the field stays on the field.

Looking out from Table Mountain
in South Africa.

I'LL BE SEEING YOU ...

By Matthew Mott

When Roy was at the Cricket Academy in Adelaide, he and a few of the other scholars were walking through Rundle Mall one day when they came upon a stand selling raffle tickets. Depending on who you talk to, the person staffing it was either a pretty young thing, or a kindly, grandmotherly type. Anyway, Roy bowled up, bought some tickets and then asked when the prize was being drawn.

'It's being drawn on the 31st of this month,' came the reply.

'Well,' said a confident Roy to the lady and the other blokes he was with, 'I guess I should expect a call on the 32nd then, shouldn't I.'

Matthew says: 'This is one of those stories that has got better with the telling over the years, but Roy will admit that he uttered the punchline!'

CHAPTER 7

THE ROAD TO ABERGAVENNY

My childhood cricketing heroes were Viv Richards, Richie Richardson and Kim Hughes, in that order. Two West Indians and an Aussie. I feel Australian in my bones, my earliest memories are of Australia and, apart from a tape that Dad has of a sweet-voiced little English five-year-old reciting 'The Tale of Jeremy Fisher' by Beatrix Potter, I sound as Aussie as a cow cocky from Cunnamulla. So you can imagine my surprise at being hauled before the Gloucestershire County Cricket Club's Chief Executive Officer, Phillip August, and asked to choose one over the other.

Unbeknown to me, I'd arrived in England during a period when the debate over selecting 'foreign' cricketers was at fever pitch. The likes of Craig White, Martin McCague, Andy Caddick and later Jason Gallian and Alan Mullally opted to play for England, despite having connections to Australia or New Zealand. Naturally, I wanted to be able to take advantage of my situation, gaining valuable match experience in the English County competition, but when it came to the national squad there was no question: I still called Australia home. Of course, the English didn't quite see it that way.

In July 1995 I got to play against my number two childhood hero, Richie Richardson, when Gloucestershire took on the visiting West Indian team in Bristol. Richie was captain and led his sensational team (which included Brian Lara) to a seven-wicket win. I'd been batting most of my career in a floppy hat to emulate Richie and was still going without a helmet during my first few seasons for Queensland before finally opting for the safer option.

Going to England was a good move as it turned out. In August 1995 I travelled with Gloucestershire to play Glamorgan in the bustling town of Abergavenny on the border between Wales and England. Over the course of the game, there were a few dirty looks and harsh words about my stance on playing for Australia, but ultimately it didn't matter. Although my recollection is hazy, the record books state I hit 20 sixes, including 16 in my first innings of 254. Both were records, with the previous marks being 15 in an innings and 17 in a match. It was my 20th first-class game and I had turned 20 in June.

The ground certainly contributed to the haul. It wasn't the biggest and the wicket was closest to the clubhouse side, meaning one boundary was quite long and the other was a lot closer. There was also a bit of a kink in the boundary at mid-on which made it a lot easier to reach. Glamorgan made 334 in the first dig and we were in strife at 5-79 when I got to the crease. In some ways, it was a demo version of how I should play because I got set first and just kept going and going once I started. Our wicketkeeper, Richard Williams, and I put on 213 for the sixth wicket and we ended up scoring 461.

I remember being tired but thrilled that everything had come together – the challenge was now to repeat it. Being young and confident, I thought I had it in the bag.

Glamorgan came back with a big second-innings effort of 471, but Javagal Srinath produced an exceptional effort with the ball to take 9-76 to give him the extraordinary match figures of 13-150, a performance that in any other game would have captured the headlines. I had another bat, scoring 76 and adding to the sixes total, but the match ended in a draw with Gloucestershire finishing at 9-293.

Hitting balls out of the ground is a magical sensation – there's a split second when you've got fear and excitement competing before you realise the ball's gone the journey and you're not going to get out. But for those on the other side of the fence, it can be quite a different experience.

> **Hitting balls out of the ground is a magical sensation – there's a split second when you've got fear and excitement competing before you realise the ball's gone the journey and you're not going to get out.**

Earlier in that season at Gloucestershire, we fronted up against Sussex at Hove. I was not out overnight and when we resumed the following morning, the outfield was still very dewy. Sussex's opening bowler, the former West Indian all-rounder Franklyn Stephenson, served me up a short one outside off-stump, and I cut it fiercely into the air over point. The ball hit the outfield and skidded off over the fence before cannoning into a female spectator's head. I could hear the impact from the middle – it was sickening. Our physio dashed over to help her and she was taken off to get checked out. Fortunately, apart from a badly bruised cheekbone and a black eye, she was okay, so much so that she returned later that day with an icepack and sat back in the very same seat to watch the rest of the match. Well, you can guess what happened. Batting from the other end, I swept a ball off the spinner, and hit her again! This time, it got her on the full on the thigh. I couldn't get over to her quickly enough, but thankfully she was okay, although shaken. I can't imagine what the odds are of this happening but I wish Ladbrokes had been running a book on it and I'd had a piece of the action. I sent her a note and some flowers at the end of play – she deserved something nice after the day she'd had!

I've hit a few people since as well – a sightscreen attendant at Lancashire in 2005 and a lady in Perth a few years ago who was reading a book. I lifted one over mid-on and the ball went right over the top of the book and hit her in the chest. I bolted over to make sure she was okay and luckily she was, but you do worry about spectators, particularly little kids or older people who mightn't be watching or who can't take evasive action. I've yelled out for people to look out when I've been fielding and someone has hit one into the crowd. With Twenty20 growing in popularity and more sixes being hit, I reckon it won't be too long before cricket grounds will have to start issuing warnings.

Not long after the Glamorgan game, I had a dose of my own medicine. But these salvos weren't on the field – the eligibility question just wasn't going to go away quietly. The ACB were of the view that because I'd played Under-19s for Australia, I was already tied to them, based on an International Cricket Council (ICC) ruling. To the ACB it was simple: if I played for England, I wasn't going to play for Australia. However the ICC argued that their decision was not retrospective, and so the English Cricket Board felt justified in bringing the matter to a head. Towards the end of August, which was the tail end of the English summer, I learned that I had been judged the Cricket Writers' Club Young Cricketer of the Year, an accolade presented annually since 1950 to English players. If you look back through the previous winners, it is almost a 'Who's Who' of English Test cricket, with the likes of Peter May, Fred Trueman, Colin Cowdrey, Geoff Boycott, Tony Greig, Derek Underwood, Alan Knott, Ian Botham, David Gower, Mike Gatting, Mike Atherton and Nasser Hussain. At the awards dinner, I managed to make a very short acceptance speech in which I basically tried not to say anything.

I was talking regularly to Mum and Dad who knew where I stood, and I had a few chats with Jack Russell as well. Jack would have dearly loved it if I had agreed to play for England but he never put any pressure on me. He did give me a beautiful painting of an elephant that he'd done (which occupies pride of place in my home), but it was a straight swap – I gave him the bat that scored the world record in Abergavenny, which he has displayed in his art gallery.

A week after the Cricket Writers' Club dinner, England selected me for the England 'A' tour of Pakistan. Gloucestershire were also

keen for me to stay on after scoring nearly 1400 runs for them and put together a financially attractive three-year deal. In an ideal world, I would have played for Queensland, and hopefully Australia, during the Australian summer and returned to play English County cricket each off-season. But at the time, that just wasn't possible and I had to choose one or the other. People told me if I stayed in England, I'd have benefits and money, but the lifestyle just wasn't me. You do things for financial gain at the end of your career, when you might go and play somewhere and put away a nest egg, but not at the beginning. Playing sport for your country was what I'd always wanted to do and my country was Australia. I just happened to be born in England.

Nevertheless, I hedged my bets, declining the England selectors' invitation but at the same time asking Gloucestershire whether they were prepared to offer me the three-year deal regardless. Again, I hoped things might sort themselves out before I came back for the 1996 season. But it wasn't to be.

I was portrayed as a mercenary for wanting to have my cake and eat it, mainly because I'd never denied that playing in England was largely for two reasons – cricket experience and making a living. But when it came down to brass tacks and I was forced to make a decision – to put my money where my mouth was, so to speak – there was no contest. In September 1995 I went home to take my chances with the mighty Queensland Bulls.

CHAPTER 8

A PRETTY GOOD IMPRESSION

While Geoff Boycott was hardly the most attacking player on the pitch, he more than made up for it in his subsequent role as a television commentator. Geoff was entertaining, opinionated and immediately recognisable in the box, and during my early years in England his broad Yorkshire accent really stuck in my head. Every so often I'd hear myself describing a 'creek-it' shot as 'roobish' or noting that someone's suggestion was 'daft' and made 'nowt' sense. After a while, I could do a passable impression and would make it a bit of a dressing-room feature as I moved around the English County scene. You encounter a stack of accents playing County cricket, and of course the locals never miss a chance to give you heaps about yours, so I had to learn a way of getting them back. I reckon it's common to a lot of sports – in every team there's usually someone who can do accents – it's almost always done in good fun and can be a circuit breaker when things aren't going well out on the paddock. Mahbo can do some beauties (his impersonations of rugby league callers are legendary) while Motty and I can sound like a right old pair of Yorkshiremen or Lancastrians when we get going.

But back in September 1995, I needed a lot more than funny voices to save my situation. After the hullabaloo of my first season in England, I suspected Gloucestershire were going to pull the pin and, if they didn't, the Test and County Cricket Board were likely to enforce their stance on representative cricket and make it impossible for me to return. Going home at the end of the season meant I had at least six months to get myself sorted out before I had to worry about my future, or lack of one, in the UK.

I began the 1995/96 Aussie season with a small but important milestone – my first game at the Gabba. It was a tour match against South Africa's Western Province and, while the performances were only fair, walking onto the turf as a Queensland representative was something I took enormous pride in. At the time the ground was being transformed into a modern stadium, but there was still a hill and the one-day games and Sheffield Shield matches I played there early in the season were pure magic.

Following these games, I trekked north to play a couple of matches against Sri Lanka in Mackay and Cairns, and it was during a game in the latter city that I first encountered a young spinner known as 'the rubber-band man'. From the outset, Muttiah Muralitharan bamboozled pretty much everyone – even a player as experienced as Allan Border. AB was batting in what would turn out to be his last season for the Bulls, and I think it's fair to say he found Murali a little hard to pick. After going for and then missing the first few balls, AB

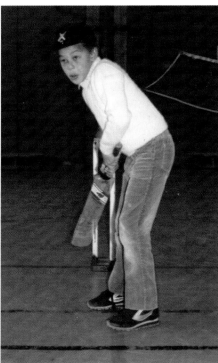

Top left: Getting bat on ball in the backyard in Geelong aged two. I favoured the floppy hat even then. (Courtesy Symonds family) **Top right:** Indoors in Ballarat in 1983 with my first 'autograph' bat – a Symonds Junior. Dig the cords, man. (Courtesy Symonds family) **Bottom left:** Standing tall with a maroon cap and a well-protected Symonds Tusker in Charters Towers after selection in the Queensland Under-13 team in 1987. (Courtesy Symonds family) **Bottom right:** Hitting the big time with the Queensland Bulls. Looks like that one was out of the middle. (Courtesy Sporting Images)

Zinc, helmet but no dreads – playing for Queensland in my formative years in the 1990s. Some 'interesting' shots are on display, and I'm not talking about the photographer's work.
(Courtesy Duane Hart/Sporting Images)

Top left: All dressed up in my Australian Under-19 blazer prior to the tour of India in March 1994. (Courtesy Symonds family)
Top right: My first season with Gloucestershire and first visit from Mum and Dad – I'll confess I was very glad to see them! (Courtesy Symonds family) **Bottom left:** Adam Dale and I shivering in the 1998 Scottish summer. (Courtesy Symonds family) **Bottom right:** Roy and Sunshine – aka yours truly and Kevin Curyer at the Australian Under-17 team announcement after the national championships in 1991/92. (Courtesy Symonds family)

Top left: Getting up close and personal with the Pura Milk Cup in 2000. (Courtesy Bob Jones Photography)

Top right: While clearly a fan of the big sunnies during the day games at the Gabba (top, right), the Richie Richardson look (middle, right) still came out occasionally during the Mercantile Mutual Cup. (Courtesy Duane Hart/Sporting Images)

Right: The 1999/2000 Pura Milk Cup championship Queensland Bulls team in full voice at Allan Border Field. (Courtesy Bob Jones Photography)

Top: The Aussie team in Sri Lanka on the 2004 tour after Warney took his 500th Test wicket.
(Courtesy Symonds family)

Middle left: Roy, Pup and Punter – aka myself, Michael Clarke and Ricky Ponting – wind down after a one-dayer.
(Courtesy Symonds family)

Middle right: Gilly and I kick back with a few well-earned coldies.
(Courtesy Symonds family)

Left: Pulling on the baggy green – cheers all round I say!
(Courtesy Symonds family)

Right: On our wedding day in April 2004.

(Courtesy Jamie Hanson/ NewsPix)

Below: Yours truly, Brooke, our dog named 'Roy' and a beaut mangrove jack.

(Courtesy Symonds family)

Top: I love my footy and rarely miss an opportunity to see the Brisbane Broncos play. When I'm really lucky, I get invited to go backstage to catch up with champions like Darren Lockyer afterwards. This was taken in April 2000. (Courtesy Symonds family) **Bottom:** After my Test debut in Galle in Sri Lanka, some, um, bronzed Aussies got together to celebrate our win and sing 'Under The Southern Cross I Stand' (Courtesy Symonds family)

Top: With the Bulls after winning a Suncorp-Metway (or as I once called it Sunway-Metcorp) Challenge one-dayer against Pakistan at the Gabba in 2000. (Courtesy Queensland Cricket)

Above (left): A fresh-faced pair! Damien Martyn and I get ready to brave the chill during the Australia 'A' tour of Scotland and Ireland in 1998. (Courtesy Symonds family)

Above (middle): Receiving my Bulls jumper from Queensland and Australian Rugby League legend Allan Langer at the 1998 season launch. 'Alf' was a pretty handy cricketer himself before turning his talents to footy. (Courtesy Bob Jones Photography)

Above (right): The first public performance of 'Geoff Boycott' at the 1998 Bulls season launch. Unusually, Mahbo was playing the straight man in this routine. (Courtesy Bob Jones Photography)

Right: Dipping into the wisdom of Rex Hunt while Kasper pretends to read something serious during an away trip with the Bulls. (Courtesy Symonds family)

walked down the wicket and said to his batting partner, 'This bloke, he's bowling leggies, right?' The yarn's got better with the telling over the years, but there was no doubting the trickiness of facing the rubber-band man and the effect he had, and continues to have, on the game.

Sri Lanka's all-guns-blazing style of cricket that had won a World Cup in 1996 meant attacking batsmen were required in response, and I was rapt to be selected for the Mercantile Mutual Cup championship team with the Bulls. Unfortunately, my enthusiasm didn't translate into spectacular performances and by season's end I yet again felt like I hadn't quite lived up to people's expectations. My patchy form didn't seem to worry Gloucestershire and against all odds I secured a three-year deal and returned for my second stint in 1996. Although I scored around 1000 runs during the season, a few of my team-mates were still upset about my status as an Australian playing in England. After another round of wrangling, it seemed I was going to be allowed to keep playing there, but only as long as the Australian selectors didn't want me for anything else …

Well, you guessed it, soon after they did. I'd bobbed up on their radar after Queensland's second Sheffield Shield match of the season when I scored my maiden hundred against a full-strength NSW team at Bankstown Oval. It was one of those knocks that seemed to pass in a blur, although I do remember running out Greg Matthews in their second innings. In the Queensland Youth squads we'd practised this particular move – diving full-length for the ball and getting up quickly to throw the stumps down – and as I got older and stronger, it became a lot easier. When it works, you dive onto your stomach and in the same movement as the ball hits your hands, you 'surf' up through your torso onto your knees, take aim and let fly. It's very satisfying. When it works. When it doesn't you eat dust.

On the back of this spurt of good form, I was picked for the Prime Minister's XI to play the West Indies and Australia 'A' to play Pakistan, which meant I got to spend a bit of time talking to Courtney Walsh about the implications for Gloucestershire of my national selection prospects. Even though he was a stalwart of the County, he understood my ambition to make my way in the Australian system and I knew I had his best wishes. As it turned out, my inclusion in the 'A' team against the Windies was a false start – or a stay of execution if you were from Gloucester – because I was 12th man, but just a few weeks later I walked out onto the SCG for the game against Pakistan as a bona fide Aussie 'A' player, which effectively spelt the end of my County career. I didn't return to the UK until I was picked up by Kent in 1999.

The 1996/97 season ended on an unexpected high: the Bulls were supposed to be in the hunt against the Warriors in Perth, with the home side only needing to draw to claim the title, but a bit of magic from Tank Barsby, Stuart Law, Michael 'Kasper' Kasprowicz and Adam 'Chippin' Dale, coupled with some good old Buck mystique, saw us spring an upset. After 69 years out in the cold, we'd come home victorious not once but twice in three years. Even though the 1994/95 Shield win was the one that stopped a State, for me, our triumph in Perth was just as momentous. Motty scored a respectable 86 in our first innings to help set up our challenge. Tank was playing his 100th Shield game and despite battling illness, produced 67 and 111, pulling off some absolute screaming catches at short leg. Stuey Law hit 70 in each innings while Kasper and Chippin took eight and nine wickets respectively. If it hadn't been for a mighty 152 from Tom Moody in the Western Australia second dig, we would have wrapped up the game early on the final day. I contributed a couple of 30s, but in the end it was mostly a vote for Buck's philosophy that a well-prepared team with plenty of self-belief will always be tough to beat.

◀▮▮▶

Winning something that big so early in my career meant a lot to me, and even as I've moved more into the Australian team ranks, I've always tried to keep in touch with my mates in the Bulls and Gold Coast teams. It annoys me if players forget where they come from, and this was something that was drilled into us by the more senior players when we came into the side. Now that I'm classed as an 'old hand', I'm a bit of a dressing-room tyrant if I reckon someone is losing sight of how they got to where they are. Of course I'm far from perfect, but I do pride myself on being available for selection for the Dolphins or the Bulls anytime I am fit and able.

The footnote to our WACA heroics came two years later when the tables were neatly turned and the Warriors came to the Gabba and nailed us. That game featured one of the most pointless centuries I have ever scored. We were fighting our way back after a poor start to our first innings and although I scored a hundred in the second session, I got out in the last over before the tea break to a shot I needn't have played. I was filthy on myself for not batting for the team because the runs I scored were worthless if I wasn't out there to take us through to stumps. Another hard lesson, learned the hard way.

◀▮▮▶

I began this chapter highlighting the fun I've had mimicking Geoff Boycott, but I think the best impersonation I've ever done was when I tried to become a pace bowler. Now 'pace bowler' can mean anything from express to trundler, but it definitely does not apply to spinners, which I'd been since my junior days. Don't get me wrong, I used to enjoy terrorising the boys in the nets at training from time to time by steaming in with a new ball – I'd get in early and pinch one before the quicks had finished stretching – but Buck and the Queensland selectors suggested I ought to seriously consider adding another string to my bow. Buck's line of thinking was that I should add medium-pace bowling to batting, slow bowling and fielding, and frankly, I could see no real counter-argument, other than I might occasionally get a bit mixed up.

I'd always got on well with Chippin, even though I used to make his life hell on occasions – honestly, if the fish bit as well as Chippin did, I'd never miss out on a feed! But as a bowler, he was an ideal teacher, mainly because he was a fair bit slower than the likes of Bic or Kasper, and he could really swing the ball.

I was a diligent student – even Chippin admits that – but I rarely took what you'd call a 'scientific' approach. Chippin suggested I bowl off ten paces – which was about the length of his run-up – and so we worked it out before a one-day game against the Canberra Comets at Manuka Oval. It only took about five minutes and has served me well ever since, even though the mental adjustment is often harder than the physical. I've worked on my bowling over the years and am probably at a point where I'm used more often these days off the longer run. I've learned to swing the ball and can get the odd one to go 'Irish' with reverse swing, which has come in handy on occasion.

Even if I'll never trouble the opening bowlers, I've always got my impression of a former English Test opener to fall back on!

Trying for a bit of swing.

SHAKE, RATTLE AND ROLL

By Michael Kasprowicz

Before a game at the Gabba, Geoff Foley came into the dressing room and asked the team if it was okay to bring in a guest. Geoff explained that this guest was a member of the Queensland Deaf Cricket team and was keen to see how the Bulls prepared for a match. There was general agreement among the group before Roy chipped in from the corner of the room: 'It's okay but only if he brings in one of those balls they play with.'

Someone asked him, 'Which ball is that, Roy?'

'You know, the one that rattles ...'

CHAPTER 9

SALT AND PEPPER

When I first made it into the Queensland Sheffield Shield squad in 1993, Matthew 'Haydos' Hayden had already established himself as a rising star, and a strong personality to boot. After a bit of circling – like a pair of dogs that aren't sure whether they should get on, or just get snapping – we soon worked out that we had a lot in common. If you've got this far, you can guess that I'm talking mainly about fishing, though that's by no means everything. We've built a strong friendship, and over the years he's been a great help in my life and with my game. He's also introduced me to a number of people from up north who have since become good mates: in particular his big brother, Gary, who's a teacher; the Fortini family, especially Anthony Fortini (or 'Yogi' as we call him); and Alan Parry, who runs Parry Nissan in Townsville.

As a youngster in Charters Towers, apart from sport and fishing, I'd also enjoyed a spot of feral pig hunting using a rifle or

Fly fishing with Haydos in
South Africa.

bow and arrow. It might sound like a dangerous thing for a kid to get up to on a weekend, but in rural Queensland it's pretty common, and we always took gun safety seriously. Up around Ingham, which is on the Herbert River in the north-eastern part of the state, they do it a bit more 'personally' – using dogs, knives and brute strength – which makes for a much more exciting experience, though it's definitely not one for the squeamish!

These days, I love nothing more than getting away after a tour or in the off-season and setting my compass for Ingham. They reckon there are more than eight million feral pigs running around Cape York alone and they cause havoc on farms, trampling crops and damaging fencing, so the locals are more than happy for them to be culled. Hunting is primal stuff and a great stress buster: you've got your swag, flannelette shirts, footy shorts, Akubra or John Deere cap, and a pig dog – 'Mac' in my case, who was a champion – and you just 'go native' for a few weeks, as Haydos likes to say. You've got to keep your wits about you and it certainly takes a bit of skill: once the dogs corner a boar, you do your best to get it over quickly. In and out. A quick kill is the most humane way to do it; it increases your chances of selling the carcass for a few bob – apparently they're a highly-prized gourmet meal in Europe and parts of Asia – and it also means your dogs are less likely to get hurt. As a bonus, you might also get a photo of you and your trophy published in Australia's only quarterly magazine devoted entirely to feral pig hunting – the ever popular *Bacon Busters*!

The Bulls coaching assistant Justin Sternes, who came on board in 2000, let slip that he and his brother Damien were also fairly handy at the pig-hunting caper, so after exchanging a few photos of big black boars, I was on my way to Tara in western Queensland. While there wasn't $20 on offer this time, my knee was in good nick and I managed to catch a little piglet. I took him home to the Gold Coast hinterland and intended to fatten him up for Christmas lunch. Brooke and I did a pretty good job, but when the dinner table eventually beckoned, we came over all reluctant. The piggy must have got wind of his stay of execution, because the carving knives weren't even sharpened before he broke out of his pen and high-tailed it into the scrub. I kept an eye on the local papers for a while after that to see if there were any sightings, but there's been no trace of our escapee since ...

While Haydos and I have had a lot of fun off the field, his help in getting my cricket back on track, particularly during the turbulent mid-1990s, has been invaluable.

I didn't need to be Einstein to work out that opportunities were beginning to open up for me in 1997. The Australian Cricket Board (ACB) had just introduced their central contract system, and after being part of the Bulls' Sheffield Shield win in Perth the previous season, I was lucky enough to land what they call a 'developmental deal' for 1997/98.

I'd well and truly embraced the North Queensland lifestyle by this stage, and as it was the off-season, I didn't think twice about dropping into Queensland Cricket Headquarters in Brisbane in my four-wheel drive ute with Mac on the back, wearing my Parramatta Rugby League footy shorts, blue Jackie Howe singlet, Akubra hat and best thongs. I'd come from putting some crab pots out so I probably had a whiff of bait on me as well, but the staff at Queensland Cricket were used to me coming and going in this fashion and didn't bat an eyelid. But on this particular day, when I arrived, instead of scribbling my name on a few forms at reception, I was whisked down the corridor to the office of the Chief Executive Graham 'Dicko' Dixon. Interesting. When I entered the room, sitting next to Dicko was none other than Malcolm Speed (former Melbourne lawyer, now ACB CEO), immaculately turned out in an expensive suit, freshly pressed shirt, tie and very polished shoes. The two men were looking patiently over my paperwork. Now Dicko wouldn't have minded if it had just been me and him, but adding the big boss into the mix made things just a little uncomfortable.

It turns out Malcolm had wanted to meet each of the players the ACB was signing up in order to outline the obligations of the contract system and explain how the payments would work. I reckon he also wanted to suss each of us out. The deal made sense to me, but as soon as the speech was over and I'd signed on the dotted line, I was out of there. Dicko later told me that after I'd left, Malcolm merely raised an eyebrow, as if to say: 'Okay ... there goes ten grand – better keep an eye on *that* one.'

◄▮►

Despite having the confidence of the ACB, my 1997/98 season started poorly as I struggled to marry the attacking style of cricket I liked to play with the consistency that was expected of me. In my mind the two seemed incompatible, and my indecision only added to the pressure. The one-day games – ordinarily my favourite cricketing arena – were proving especially frustrating and while there had been no direct threat, I could hear the selectors' axes being sharpened. Haydos and I were really good mates by this stage ('Salt' and 'Pepper' as some of the dressing-room wags had dubbed us) and unbeknown to me, he decided to intervene on my behalf, seeking out the Queensland chairman of selectors, Max Walters, for a bit of a chin-wag. In my opinion, Max was an outstanding chairman – intelligent and with a knack of looking beyond the stats when it came to picking players – and he didn't get too emotionally involved in the selection process, although he enjoyed the victories and lamented the losses like any of us.

Haydos didn't beat about the bush. He asked Max point blank whether they were going to drop me. Without giving any guarantees, Max explained that while he'd like to see me scoring more runs, he was of the view that I was a 'match winner' and it was worth running up a few dry gullies in exchange for the day when things would click and a win we really needed might jump into our laps.

Mission accomplished, Haydos then turned to the other three things he thought would help my game: practice, practice and more practice. For the remainder of the season, whenever we weren't at regular Bulls training, we were at the Gabba's indoor nets. I reckon we wore out some of the bowling machines we were there for that long. We might have even talked more about batting than fishing during that period, though I couldn't say for sure.

Buck, who had been positive about my form and was always encouraging, knew exactly where Haydos was taking me, and just before Christmas 1997, I got the first signs that things might be starting to come good. It was another of the day/night Sheffield Shield games, this time in Perth against the Warriors, and despite the conditions being tough, I managed 88 when we were in a tight spot.

After that game, it was like the brakes had been taken off and the petrol tank filled with high-octane fuel – the rest of the season passed in a blur of centuries as Haydos and I reaped the benefits of our earlier work. I got a hundred in the next game against Victoria, one against Tasmania and then another two in each innings against

South Australia. Each time, the runs came freely, but there was the welcome addition of patience that had evolved from the sessions with Haydos. He finished as Queensland's leading runs-scorer, with just over 900, and I ended up with just over 800 with an average of nearly 50. Good numbers, made even better by the fact that the Bulls defeated NSW at the SCG to win the Mercantile Mutual Cup.

———

The 1998 off-season loomed large, and with no English County contract forthcoming, I took some time off and set about enjoying the great outdoors for a couple of months. The Commonwealth Games were on in Malaysia in September of that year, with cricket included for the first time, and while I'd been a street corner tip to tour, I didn't make it, much to the detriment of the mud crabs and fish at Jacobs Well. Cricket's inclusion at the Games was a one-off as it turned out, and Australia ended up with the silver medal.

A knee injury to all-rounder Tom Moody ruled him out of the next international commitment – the Wills Cup in Bangladesh in October – and put me in the frame. After tying my colours to Australia's mast a few seasons earlier, I was finally about to get the chance to raise them high. Of course, when the call came from the national selectors, I was out fishing and uncontactable. In those days, I had a suspicion of mobile phones and viewed them as something that I could easily do without. I held out for a fair while too before finally succumbing and joining the rest of the civilised world. Anyway, Dad took the call and both he and Mum were just about as excited as I was.

The Wills Cup was a mini-World Cup tournament that the ICC was running to raise funds to better develop cricket in Bangladesh.

Australia had been in Pakistan for the Test series, which they won 1-0, the first time in 39 years they had triumphed there. The one-day players met them in Bangladesh for the tournament, which was a knockout format. I didn't play in Australia's only game, a loss to India, so I had to wait for a little longer to get the feel of an Aussie cap.

In Pakistan, I looked on enviously as Australia won the first two games before Steve Waugh finally gave me the news I'd been waiting for: I was going to play.

Gaddafi Stadium in Lahore (so named after the Libyan dictator) was packed; clearly my debut was not going to be a low-key affair. Even though I'd been rooming with Boof Lehmann and had the advantage of his experience about what to expect, I was still nervous, no two ways about it. Walking out onto the ground, the noise was deafening – there was banging of bottles, chanting, whistling and cheering. The pitch was as flat as the floor and I bowled two overs for 14. There were balls flying everywhere as Yousef Youhanna scored a ton and Ijaz Ahmed whacked 111 off 109 balls. Pakistan raced to 315 off their 50 overs and I thought to myself, 'This is interesting. Hold onto your hat!'

Somehow we managed to turn things around and ended up getting the runs in what was a world record chase. Punter and Gilly had crackers and both belted hundreds. I was padded up and rearing to go but Michael Bevan went in and got us home, so it wasn't to be.

Even though I'd have loved to have been more involved, it was actually a bit of a relief. I knew I was either going to be under the hammer because wickets had fallen or coming in at the end needing to smack them around to get across the line. It was only the briefest taste of what was to come, but I was hooked.

CHAPTER 10

SURVIVAL INSTINCTS

Throughout my cricketing career, and my life in general, I've frequently relied on my intuition, or what they sometimes call 'instinct'. Indeed, one of the most common descriptions of my game is 'instinctive'. No arguments there: give me a simple, clearly defined task and let me get the job done. It sounds as though I'm stating the obvious, but I really play my best when I'm fit, have practised plenty and my mind is clear. Throw in a bit of pressure, particularly when the team's in strife, and I often find that little bit extra. Perhaps laziness also has something to do with it – sometimes I need to have my back against the wall with the easy options exhausted before I really step up.

Just after Christmas in 1999, Brooke and I took a mid-season holiday on North Stradbroke Island, in Moreton Bay off Brisbane, with Haydos and his wife, Kellie. It was the ideal way to unwind – camping, fishing, relaxing and seeing in the New Year with good mates. Haydos and I had gone halves in fixing up his old man's boat, an orange Haines 16-footer that had been up at their farm at Kingaroy and, determined to make our mark on the fish of the new millennium, we took to the seas on 2 January with a friend of Haydos', Trent Butler, who was writing for *Queensland Fishing Monthly* at the time.

We left around dawn and headed for the Amity Point Bar. I was driving and was using our GPS to follow the 'bread crumbs' – the trail out that we had followed over the past few days – and although it was getting light, my direction was out that day and by the time we got close to getting through the sand bar and out into the open sea, we were probably 50 metres off where we should have been.

Big mistake.

Out of nowhere, a set of three huge waves stood up right in front of us. I looked over at Haydos to see what he reckoned we should do. 'Give it a gutful,' was his advice, so I did, and managed to get airborne over the first wave, but we landed heavily and dunked the motor, snuffing it out. A second later, the next wave hit us and pushed us half side-on, filling the boat up to our calves. We tried to re-start the engine but there was no spark so we did a quick check of the battery and fuel line to see if anything had come loose but there was nothing wrong as far as we could see. Could we have missed something when we fixed up the boat? Nah. Anyway, we were now totally side-on to the third wave and it was fairly clear to all aboard we were going for a dip. Although there was no time to get the life jackets, just as we were about to take the plunge over the side, Haydos coolly grabbed his sunnies and tucked them into his togs.

Moments later the third big wave swamped us and our boat began to sink below the surface, ending up seconds later with only its nose showing. There would have been a five-knot current tugging us out to sea, but at least we could see the beach, which was around a kilometre away. We decided we'd better swim for it and Haydos took off like Kieren Perkins with Trent and me following in his wake. I'm a reasonable swimmer, but from the outset I could tell that Trent was going to bring up third spot in our little ocean dip. He was wearing the world's biggest pair of boardshorts and they were dragging him under so I told him to ditch them to make things easier. He said they were a Christmas present from his missus and there was no way he was going to chuck them. Needless to say, after a few hundred metres of swimming across the current in the waves, he was cooked.

For those who don't know the waters of Moreton Bay and North Stradbroke Island, I'm not exaggerating when I say there are some nasty critters lurking in those depths. There's been more than a few surfers and swimmers taken by sharks over the years and with a lot of amateurs and professionals fishing the area, you know that where there are little fish, there will also be big fish. To make matters worse, when our boat was hit, our buckets of bait and fish oil and other tasty stuff had gone into the drink and were now floating all around us …

I was confident that Haydos and I were going to make it to shore, but I was getting worried about Trent. If you put someone in

For those who don't know the waters of Moreton Bay and North Stradbroke Island, I'm not exaggerating when I say there are some nasty critters lurking in those depths.

a pool and ask them to swim a kilometre, it's most likely they'll be okay, but add in waves and a current – not to mention the threat of sharks and other nasties – and that one kilometre can feel more like ten. Haydos and I yelled at Trent to try breaststroke or sidestroke and tread water to catch his breath when he was starting to knock up. Fortunately the water wasn't too cold, but by the time we got about halfway, Trent was on struggle street. At one point, he didn't think he could go any further and so we gave him the choice of trying to swim back to the boat and hanging onto it until someone came, or letting us help him swim into the beach. Haydos was looking at me with a funny expression but wasn't saying anything. He told me later that he was thinking of knocking Trent out so we could float him in! Anyway, Trent wasn't having a bar of going back to the boat so we got him settled and kept moving. We were going slowly though and making sure we stayed right on his shoulder, because if he had gone under and we weren't close, I reckon he would have been a goner.

By this time a call must have gone out because there were two or three pro fishing boats circling in the distance. I'm sure they could see our debris floating all around, and we could see them looking for us, scooting in and out of waves and putting themselves at risk, but I don't think they could see us even though Haydos and I were waving and shouting as we bobbed up and down in the swell. We were inching closer to the shore though, and after a few exploratory efforts putting a foot down, I finally hit the bottom, just behind where the waves were breaking. I told Trent that I could touch and, because he was knackered and not really thinking clearly, he stopped swimming and went to put both feet on the bottom. Well, he must have been in a deep spot because he went down like a stone.

Haydos and I dived under and grabbed him under the arms, reefing him back to the surface and swimming him in as best we could for the last couple of hundred metres. We reached a sandbar and then had to get through a deep gutter and finally got to the beach break where we could start to walk in. We all collapsed on the sand and Haydos and I just sat there looking at each other, processing what had happened.

Then he reached into his togs, took out his sunglasses and put them back on.

After our little incident, our Bulls team-mates dubbed us 'Skipper' and 'Gilligan' for the remainder of the summer and even presented us with floaties and a rubber tyre tube before our next game …

◼▐▌▐◼

I've always considered my pastimes risky but not overly dangerous. Plumbers, builders, teachers and doctors all do the sort of things I like doing to unwind, but I guess few of them have Cricket Australia player contracts that forbid taking part in 'extreme sports'. Our definitions of 'extreme' clearly differ, as you'd expect. And besides, you've more chance of having a car accident than getting eaten by a croc.

Nonetheless, over the years I've had to be 'creative' on occasion to avoid getting into trouble. I once rode my new quad bike into a barbed-wire fence just prior to a tour. Overnight rain had made things greasy and when I gave it some juice, the bike slipped and I collided with the strainer post and the start of the fence. I probably needed stitches in the gashes on my arm but I bandaged them up and made sure I wore long-sleeve shirts for the first week of the tour. I was lucky that time and I now realise that while it's a rush hanging off a wild bull's tail while trying to wrestle it to the ground with the help of some jackeroos, it's not the sort of thing a professional cricketer should really make a habit of.

The boating accident off Stradbroke Island came in the middle of a two-year period that was a bit like a snapshot of my career up to that point. Between 1999 and 2001 my form and results could kindly be described as 'mixed'. On one hand, I was starting to put some consistent numbers on the board for Queensland, but on the other, my international performances in the one-day arena were decidedly ordinary. And while my survival instincts had been tested and not been found wanting in the ocean, they'd need to be honed when it came to my career.

In 1999, I enjoyed a return to England to play County cricket for Kent as their overseas professional, having put the dramas of 1995 and 1996 well behind me. Kent were very welcoming and things went tidily on the field – I scored 900 first-class runs and had a bit of success in the one-day games for the Spitfires, as they were known.

When I got back to Australia, I averaged nearly 60 in first-class cricket for the Bulls during the 1999/2000 season where we won the newly-created Pura Milk Cup for the first time. That was the second first-class championship I'd been involved in after the 1996/97 Sheffield Shield win. Queensland drew the match against Victoria, with a Martin Love century and a defiant Stuart Law taking the game away from the Bushrangers. I didn't trouble the scorers in the first innings and then gave up bragging rights altogether when I became one of Matthew Mott's two victims in the second innings. And didn't I hear about that …

A beautiful cut shot.

Motty had made the move from Queensland to Victoria for the 1998/99 season in search of a more permanent first-class post and had a few good years with them before switching to NSW where he has since gone on to build a reputation as a very promising coach. I was sorry to see him leave Queensland because we'd come through a fair bit together, but I understood his reasons.

Internationally, I turned in a few handy efforts in some out-of-the-way places. In 12 months I managed a man-of-the-match effort against India in Galle in Sri Lanka (where I hit my highest score in

ODI cricket with 68 off 68 balls); played for Australia 'A' in California against India 'A'; and took on Kenya in Nairobi. Good for the passport stamp collection at the very least. I love touring and while I'm not in the Steve Waugh or Matthew Hayden class when it comes to keeping notes and soaking up the local culture, I try to get out and see as much as I can. It can be hectic though for the uninitiated – in the two and half months between August and October 1999, my schedule took me to England, Sri Lanka, back to England, the United States, Australia, Zimbabwe, and then home.

◼◖▮▶

The VB Series in 1999/2000 was against India and Pakistan, with a tour of New Zealand in February 2000, and again, while I didn't do too badly, I wasn't able to put it all together and reel off the big scores. The advice I was getting at the time from Buck and Bennett King was not to get too far ahead of myself and keep things simple, but I was a bit like the brumby that had been half broken in but would still pitch an unwary rider when they least expected it. More often than not, my role would involve coming to the crease with not many balls remaining just looking to blast as many runs as possible. There wasn't a lot of margin for error and it's easy to string together a few failures. And a few failures can quickly be seized upon as being 'out of form', which, try as you might, can seep into the sub-conscious.

I was lucky though in the 1999/2000 season to have the opportunity to pick the brains of Sachin Tendulkar, who I regard, along with Brian Lara, as one of the very best players in the world. During the tour game between Queensland and India at the Gabba, Mahbo and I sat down with Sachin to talk batting after watching him score a typically elegant 83 in their first innings. It's not something I do all that often, but with a player like Sachin, you'd be mad not to. He was quite humble but still very forthcoming: for him, it all came down to balance and keeping your head still. He's pretty short and works on the principle that if he's well balanced, even if his feet aren't completely to the ball, he can still be in control. He was spot on about keeping his head still. When I'm too keen to whack it, my head wobbles, but if I don't 'tip' it over, then I play straight, rather than across myself. I must have listened well, because when I next went out into the middle, I hit 161 off 174 balls. It was a bit like the Australian Under-19 tour a few years before because India's first innings century-maker was none other than VVS Laxman. I batted with Martin Love and he was at his unflustered best on the way to 120 as we put on a partnership of 204. Queensland ended up winning by ten wickets, with paceman Scotty Muller and spinner Matthew 'Jackpot' Anderson taking seven between them.

After a short ODI tour of South Africa in April 2000, I had a rare off-season at home, with the hunting and fishing broken up by the first winter series that the ACB had tried. It was weird playing under the roof at Docklands and while no one managed it, I think we all wondered what it would take to hit the ceiling. We had to wait until 2005 to find out when Mike Hussey turned out to be the man for that challenge with his shot in the ICC Super Series clanging off the roof.

The 2000/01 Australian season followed in a similar pattern to the previous: good runs on occasion, some decent performances for Queensland, and a place in the Australian one-day team for the series against the West Indies and Zimbabwe. I batted my best for the Bulls against Tasmania at Allan Border Field in October. Border Field is a mid-sized ground but there are some rewards for those willing to hit out, especially square of the wicket. Ricky Ponting was making one of his rare appearances for the Tigers and made up for lost time by thumping 233 against us. Tassie set us a run chase of 372 from 72 overs on the final day, and after the loss of Haydos, Mahbo and Stuart Law, the Bulls were looking shaky. Martin Love and I got a bit of momentum going and after a while, we were rolling like a Central Queensland coal train without brakes.

We really were the odd couple of batting though – me swinging hard and lifting them in the air and Lovey calmly punching them through the field – but it had the desired effect. The final scorecard showed a four-wicket win to Queensland, with an over to spare, and the victory coming in near darkness. Lovey and I put on 261 for the fourth wicket, scoring those runs off 42 overs, and including a period when we poached 100 in just 8.3 overs. Lovey finished 161 not out off 195 balls and I hit 133 off 122 balls.

That set the scene for Queensland for 2000/01, with the Bulls winning their second Pura Cup title in a row by beating the Bushrangers by four wickets at the Gabba in March. But while the boys were spraying the XXXX around, I was on the subcontinent where Australia was gearing up for the 2001 Ashes tour by staging an epic Test series with India. I couldn't get out of second gear for the One Day Internationals and didn't hit the headlines (leaving that for the likes of Haydos and VVS Laxman who produced some stunning innings across the series).

I was going to England again for the 2001 County season with Kent, but had factored in my likely selection for the one-day leg of the Ashes series. I played two tour games and five ODIs without producing anything special. My frustrations at not being able to crack this international caper were building and I was starting to think that perhaps I needed some help. Or maybe another option. Or both.

But I carried on, despite feeling increasingly out of sorts. The 2001/02 season brought another trophy for the Bulls as they completed a hat-trick of Pura Cup titles under the stewardship of Stuart Law and Bennett King. Both those blokes did their best to keep me focused during the season as my form continued to waver but in the end, the national selectors finally lost patience and I was dropped from the one-day team in January 2002. Not that there was much of a protest from the fans. In the space of a month, Australia missed the final of the VB Series and Steve Waugh was replaced as one-day captain for the subsequent tour of South Africa.

I went into the Pura Cup Final against Tasmania a confused and angry young man. Getting 91 in the first innings helped fractionally – especially when the Tigers were certain they had got me leg before wicket from the first ball I faced. A hundred would have helped my national selection cause, but it wasn't to be, and I was just glad to be able to celebrate a championship with the Bulls to help put that behind me.

ROY'S HIGHEST SCORES
FIRST CLASS

23/08/1995
COUNTY, GLOUCESTERSHIRE v GLAMORGAN, ABERGAVENNY

RUNS	BALLS	6's	STK-RT
254*	206	16	123.30

26/05/1999
COUNTY, KENT v LEICESTERSHIRE, CANTERBURY

RUNS	BALLS	6's	STK-RT
177	245	3	72.24

05/03/1998
PURA, QUEENSLAND v SOUTH AUSTRALIA, ADELAIDE

RUNS	BALLS	6's	STK-RT
163	202	3	80.69

06/11/2005
PURA, QUEENSLAND v SOUTH AUSTRALIA, ADELAIDE

RUNS	BALLS	6's	STK-RT
163	183	1	89.07

27/04/1995
COUNTY, GLOUCESTERSHIRE v SURREY, THE OVAL

RUNS	BALLS	6's	STK-RT
161*	140	4	115.00

26/11/1999
TOUR, QUEENSLAND v INDIA, BRISBANE

RUNS	BALLS	6's	STK-RT
161	173	1	93.06

09/12/1999
PURA, QUEENSLAND v WESTERN AUSTRALIA, BRISBANE

RUNS	BALLS	6's	STK-RT
158	154	1	102.60

23/06/2004
COUNTY, KENT v WARWICKSHIRE, BECKENHAM

RUNS	BALLS	6's	STK-RT
156*	167	4	93.41

WHAT'S ON THE MENU?

By Wade Seccombe

Roy and his roommate, the Bulls all-rounder Scott 'Presto' Prestwidge, were on an away trip to Adelaide a few years back. The team had trained in the morning and that meant the afternoon was free, so Roy and Presto decided to watch an in-house movie at the hotel. Presto went to the bathroom and asked Roy to choose one. While in the bathroom taking care of business, he heard Roy groaning and carrying on. When he came out, he asked Roy what the problem was.

'Oh mate, there are some sick people out there – you press 10 and you get Comedy Movies, you press 20 and you get Action Movies, you press 30 and you get Thrillers, you press 40 and you get Family Movies, but when you press 50, you get "Disabled" Adult Movies! Who the hell watches that sort of stuff?'

Wade says: 'I've since heard this story told about other cricketers, and more graphically as well, but Roy was the original innocent at large this time.'

CHAPTER 11

THE BIG SWITCH

When you're one of rugby league's most successful coaches, the last person you expect to hear from late one night is a struggling 27-year-old cricketer. But in 2002, Wayne Bennett – the legendary Brisbane Broncos, Queensland and Australian coach – was having a quiet night in front of the TV when his wife Trish sung out that an Andrew Symonds was on the blower.

For the previous 18 months I'd been edging towards a career crossroads, and towards the end of the 2001 Ashes tour, I'd tried to explain my frustrations to Buck and Steve Waugh. At the time, I didn't feel comfortable in the Australian team environment: it was a 'survival of the fittest' culture and while I understood this, I enjoy other people's success and have always prided myself on being able to help them achieve it. I don't care if it's not always reciprocated, that's not why I do it. But I did feel at that point that I was doing a lot of the giving, and that plenty of people were doing the taking,

With Darren Lockyer of
the Broncos in 2000.

and there was no acknowledgment of that. I don't know if Buck and Steve understood where I was coming from, but the point I was trying to make was that I felt that some people weren't being upfront and I was better off out of there. I told them cricket would always be my first love but that maybe it was time to cut my losses and try something new.

I still enjoyed playing with the Bulls but I knew I wasn't contributing and scoring as well as I should have been. I started to question myself and wondered whether this was as good as it was going to get. Had I reached my peak? If that was the case, then I was in for a heap of frustration as I'd not achieved nearly all that I wanted to. I began to cast about for something that would change the way I was thinking, because I didn't like things the way they were.

I'd played plenty of sports growing up and had been reasonable at soccer and hockey, playing in the Queensland Under-15 hockey team alongside future Kookaburras Baedon Choppy and Michael Brennan, but in second place after cricket had always been rugby league. I played league at All Souls in Charters Towers, union at All Saints on the Gold Coast and even made the First XV at All Saints and represented South Coast. I envied the Queensland State of Origin players because their game seemed to be the toughest and most skilful imaginable and I'd often wondered what it'd be like to pull on a Maroon jersey and run out onto Lang Park to take on NSW. I still get pretty worked up when I'm watching the games each year.

Somewhere along the line, I started to think that maybe it *was* possible to seriously give another sport a go, so I discussed with Brooke and a few other close friends and decided it was at least worth a phone call …

So I'm on the phone to Wayne Bennett and I blurt out that I want to talk to him about playing football with the Broncos.

There was a bit of a pause, as you'd expect, but rather than fall off the chair, he came back with a deadpan: 'Okay, yep, we can do that. When would suit?'

I couldn't believe it.

I met him at the Broncos' headquarters at Red Hill and I poured my heart out. He didn't bat an eyelid. He was straightforward and said he'd be happy to help if I wanted to explore the possibility. There were a few things we needed to find out, like how I'd cope with the physical contact, what my body could handle and what position I'd be best suited to. He then got me talking again as to why I was thinking the way I was, I guess so he could better understand it as well.

We agreed I could come along to a couple of training sessions. It was our cricket off-season and so I did some running around the hills at Ormeau to try to get a bit more condition under my belt. When I fronted up for my first session, it turned out my fitness was okay and I kept pace reasonably well. I also got to do a bit of ball-work with them, which gave me a clearer picture of whether I had what it took.

The next session, after the Broncos had lost on the weekend to Parramatta, was a different story. I should have twigged: before we began, Gordie Tallis came over and said, 'Mate, you've picked the wrong day to turn up. We're going to get flogged.' He was right, Wayne worked us hard and I was cooked halfway through but struggled on as best I could. We finished with a few set plays and some ball-work and I was part of the opposition for these particular drills. I was being tried as a winger so, the way training was structured, the starting fullback (which was the Queensland and

Australian star Darren Lockyer) would be back in opposition to put pressure on the tactical kickers to get their kicks in the right spots. Before we began the drill, Wayne said bluntly that if it was done right, then it was the last one for the session, but if there was a stuff-up, then we would start all over again.

On the fifth tackle, I dropped back for the kick and ran backwards and in-field to catch it, just as Locky was coming across from the middle. I thought to myself, 'I've got this one!' and leapt into the air to take the ball … at precisely the same time as Locky came barrelling in to do the same thing. We crashed straight into each other in mid-air, the ball hit my shoulder and bounced off towards the try-line and we came down in a messy heap. I looked up to see all of these Broncos players saying to themselves: 'What the f*** is he doing?' and thought, 'How am I going to get out of this one? These blokes are going to kill me!'

To his credit, Wayne walked over and said simply, 'Locky, you know that's Roy's speciality. Get out of the road next time.' And that was the end of training, but fortunately not the end of me.

I never took it any further than that, given the cricket season was approaching and the Broncos were into the business end of things. Looking back, it was probably pie in the sky stuff really. It would have been a gamble and I would have started off a long way away from the Broncos and under a fair bit of scrutiny. And if I was lacking confidence with my cricket, how was I going to handle a new sport at which I was a total novice?

The one thing it did do was provide me with a circuit-breaker and allow me to re-focus on what I wanted. And that was cricket.

To his credit, Wayne walked over and said simply, 'Locky, you know that's Roy's speciality. Get out of the road next time.'

And as it turned out, cricket wanted me, even though as I said at the beginning of this book, my selection in the 2003 World Cup squad was probably the biggest surprise of my life. That summer I'd tried being aggressive and that hadn't worked; I'd tried grinding out the innings, and that hadn't worked either, so I really didn't think I had a hope in hell. After the announcement, I told the media that that I was just pleased to be going – I would have been happy to be the stump mike if that's what they wanted – but once I got back to the dressing room after all of the attention had died away, I felt like a bit of a fraud.

As the realisation sunk in that I really was going to cricket's greatest show on earth, I started to brighten up a bit, but lurking in the back of my mind was still that feeling of 'pinch me, I'm dreaming'. Ultimately, I told myself that if it was a dream, I'd better make it one to remember when I woke up.

THE LIGHTS ARE ON ...

By Michael Kasprowicz

We were preparing for a game at the Adelaide Oval in the mid-1990s not long after the South Australian Cricket Association introduced the infamous retractable floodlight towers. Basically, when the towers were retracted, the light 'heads' would be lowered down to ground level. When we arrived, Roy noticed there was something funny about the lights, especially the one that was behind one of the hill areas.

'Geez, look at that thing,' he said. As soon as he drew our attention to the fact, it was almost a competition to see who could string him along the furthest. Trevor Barsby jumped to tell him that they were the brand new lights that had just been installed.

Roy had a good look at them, and was clearly concerned. 'It's not going to be easy fielding out there at night – you'd be looking straight at them because they are down so low.'

Tank then told him that no, they were 'special' lights and wouldn't glare at all.

Roy was still shaking his head at this perceived design flaw when he found another: 'And what about the spectators? They're going to get really hot with that behind their backs ...'

We kept him going for a while, insisting that the 'special' lights were nothing short of miraculous. I can't remember who cracked first, but it took a lot of convincing that the lights were legit.

Needless to say he was pretty happy when the SACA scrapped them a few years later and built permanent light towers. I reckon it restored his belief in the natural order of things.

RAINING FOURS AND SIXES

The Most Fours and Sixes Hit By Australian One Day International Players

RANK	1	2	3	4	5	6
4+6	1109	884	716	597	545	511
M	241	251	244	325	271	181
INN	234	245	236	288	251	177
NO	9	29	20	58	39	16
RUNS	8209	9096	8500	7569	6524	5964
4's	988	768	658	529	501	495
6's	121	116	58	68	44	16
RUNS BD	4678	3768	2980	2524	2268	2076
%BD/RUNS	56.99	41.42	35.06	33.35	34.76	34.81
BD/INN	4.74	3.61	3.03	2.07	2.17	2.89
%6/BD	10.91	13.12	8.10	11.39	8.07	3.13
	AC GILCHRIST	RT PONTING	ME WAUGH	SR WAUGH	AR BORDER	DC BOON

RAINING FOURS AND SIXES

	7	8	9	10	11	12	RANK
4+6	471	466	439	426	398	324	
M	232	118	163	200	146	117	
INN	196	114	160	174	116	115	
NO	67	12	25	49	22	6	
RUNS	6912	4129	6057	5030	3697	4357	
4's	450	416	379	404	324	302	
6's	21	50	60	22	74	22	
RUNS BD	1926	1964	1876	1748	1740	1340	
%BD/RUNS	27.86	47.57	30.97	34.75	47.07	30.76	
BD/INN	2.40	4.09	2.74	2.45	3.43	2.82	
%6/BD	4.46	10.73	13.67	5.16	18.59	6.79	
	MG BEVAN	**ML HAYDEN**	**DM JONES**	**DR MARTYN**	**A SYMONDS**	**GR MARSH**	

CHAPTER 12

THE WORLD CUP

'Andrew Symonds is the new man out in the middle of the Wanderers ground for Australia. His average is 23.8 – it's not bad. It's higher than I thought it was going to be, to be totally honest. Best of 68, but in recent times it has been lean pickings. Batting at six in this match – no Darren Lehmann and no Michael Bevan ...'

– Mark Taylor commentating for Fox Sports

Not the most inspiring intro, but I wasn't the most inspiring batsman at that point – I'd averaged only single figures in my last international series and Tubby can be forgiven for sounding dubious about the man who had come to the crease to help rescue Australia.

I've been asked a few times about that game – what I was thinking, which shot was my favourite, how nervous I was – but to be honest, there are big chunks that I simply can't remember. It's embarrassing sometimes, and all I can really offer by way of explanation is that when things work for me in the middle, I go into this zone where I focus so fiercely on each ball I become oblivious to almost everything else. The Pakistani innings is a case in point. I remember the lead-up, batting with Ricky Ponting … hitting Wasim Akram for six back over his head and then the beam ball blow-up with Waqar Younis, but that's about it.

In doing this book I sat down with a DVD and finally watched it again. It was a weird experience – even three years on I became nervous as Wassie, Shoaib Ahktar and Waqar got among us and it got closer to me going out to bat. I came to the conclusion that so much of it is just pure luck – for example, the dismissals of Matthew Hayden and Damien Martyn in consecutive balls in the tenth over of the game, both falling to inside edges off Wasim. I could have gone the same way in the 23rd when I dragged one past the stumps off Abdul 'Ratsack' Razzaq, but I didn't, and that smidgin of good fortune definitely helped my overall knock. As Tubby had noted, before the World Cup game, I'd played 55 matches with a highest score of 68 not out, an average of 23.81 and a strike-rate of 96. If I had been Pakistan, I would have been counting on knocking me over quickly, even if I managed to hit a few runs in the process.

The build-up that day was hairy enough, with wickets tumbling and my gear flying about the dressing room. There was a point where if Mahbo had fallen on the hat-trick ball, or shortly after, I would have been pulling on those socks out on the grass. I can just imagine what Tony Greig would have made of that. To reach the field, you walk through this big plexiglass tunnel that was constructed after Merv Hughes rearranged the pickets and livened up a few South African spectators on a previous tour. It feels like you're walking into a Colosseum and I remember thinking it was just like the movie *Gladiator*.

By the time Waqar had Mahbo caught behind from a nasty ball that pitched wide and seamed to put us 4-86, I was semi-composed. Nervous definitely, but in better shape than I thought I'd be. It helped that Waqar was pumped and threw down a bouncer for my first ball, which meant it was a ball I didn't have to play. Ricky Ponting was a godsend at the other end – he kept things very simple and did his best to get me to relax and play each delivery on its merits. 'Next ball, next ball,' he kept telling me. Still, to say I was scratchy early would be generous. I sparred at a couple from Ratsack but was clearly tentative. Rats is the sort of bowler who can be tricky early in your innings as he bowls straight and makes you play them. Fortunately, I kept my edges out of the way and was able to get off the mark with a boundary between cover and mid-off, following it up with another in the same over.

The ball was swinging and seaming but it was a great day for batting and both Punter and I soon settled into a rhythm. For a while there, the biggest bother were the swarms of insects that had decided to keep us company. I still don't know what they were, but if I describe them as giant ladybugs, you'll get the picture. At the halfway point, we'd put together a 40-run partnership and pushed Australia to 4-126. There were some key bowling changes made by Waqar around this time – he brought Shoaib back to get a wicket and Shahid Afridi to get through some quick overs as they had been pretty slow with their over rates and the word was that the match referees would be tough in this regard.

Shoaib was bowling as quickly as anyone, and because he was fitter back then, he was able to keep attacking for longer. I made up my mind that I'd look to play him straight and hit anything loose, but not to take him on. He'd been brought back into the attack to blast one of us and if we were able to get through him, other opportunities would no doubt present themselves as the ball got older. Afridi, on the other hand, was flying through his overs, and you've got to closely watch his quickish legbreaks early in an innings. He's got a sharp yorker and bouncer up his sleeve and mixes his pace up well so I'm always reluctant to sweep him in case he slots one of those deliveries in. He had two blokes behind square from the outset and was trying to get me cutting. That's one of my 'go-to' shots and I was keen to take the challenge.

Then disaster struck. In Shoaib's last over, we were just about through when Punter went hard at a wider delivery and got the toe end of his bat for a catch at first slip. He was disappointed but I think it only made me even more determined.

His departure brought Brad 'Barney' Hogg to the crease – the most annoying bloke in the dressing room without doubt but the ideal batting partner because he doesn't muck around and just loves to get on with the job. We were able to pinch ten runs from Afridi the next over by scoring off every ball and I finally squeezed a cut shot between his two patrolling fielders for four, which helped return some of the lost momentum. Ratsack came back into the attack in place of Shoaib and I managed to get two boundaries in that over to go past 50. By now the pitch was starting to really flatten and Pakistan were under pressure to lift the overs, so it was no surprise to see the part-time leggie Younis Khan step up to allow them to have spinners operating at both ends. One thing you don't want to have to do in a one-dayer is rush at the end of the innings, so you could understand their urgency to claw back some time.

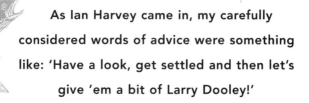

As Ian Harvey came in, my carefully considered words of advice were something like: 'Have a look, get settled and then let's give 'em a bit of Larry Dooley!'

It worked for us though. The first ball from Younis went for four and we took nine from the over, with the run-rate lifting every delivery. You could feel the balance of power slowly shifting, a bit like when you're out in a boat as the tide begins to turn and the water is swirling around as it changes direction. The 35th over was the turning point: I managed to give Afridi some tap, getting him to the boundary four times, including a mis-field from Shoaib that should have been two, and we ended up with 17 from the six balls.

Barney played beautifully that day; for a change both of us brought our brains and we were able to keep everything ticking along nicely. If only I hadn't run him out ... I cut the ball to one of the three fielders behind point and took off – Barney's quick but there was half a step of hesitation and that was it, especially when the throw was a good one to the 'keeper. We hadn't gone for a run to that area for a few overs and I think it caught him off-guard.

As Ian Harvey came in, my carefully considered words of advice were something like: 'Have a look, get settled and then let's give 'em a bit of Larry Dooley!' I don't know where I picked up that expression but I'm told it comes from an old Aussie boxer who was renowned for throwing a stack of punches. Harvs was just the bloke for a bit of 'Larry' – he's been a good mate of mine since our Academy days and is one of those players who can pull shots out of nowhere.

He got on with things from the outset, and I was stoked he was there with me when I finally neared the ton.

On 99, I played a shocker against Afridi and had to give myself a stern talking to. It must have worked because I punched the next one away through the off-side for four, which did it. Although I distinctly recall hearing Adam Gilchrist give a big 'woo-hoo' from the viewing area, there wasn't much on-field celebration – frankly I didn't really know what to do – so I just crushed Harvs and belted him in the ribs a few times, gave a quick salute and a head wobble and carried on.

Before that innings, I'd been lucky enough to get some quality work in with Tim Nielsen, our assistant coach. Timmy threw what felt like a thousand balls to me and it paid off. I got my first six in the 48th over, tonking one down the ground off Waqar, but my favourite shot of the innings, and one of the few that I remember vividly, came off Wasim from the first ball of the last over. Hitting one of the great fast bowlers back over his head for six is about as good as it gets and this particular shot was one of those glorious moments where it feels almost effortless. At 143 not out, I was walking on air, even though I was buggered. When I left the field, the boys went absolutely bozo and I know Buck had to wipe a tear away. You could see in their faces how happy and relieved they were for me.

Back home, Mum had watched the entire innings on the TV but Dad had refused. He'd taken my sister Louise to hockey training in Brisbane and it had been on the TV at the clubhouse at the State Hockey Centre. This only prompted him to head back outside, because I was about ten not out! On the way home to Ormeau, he had the car radio switched off, but even when Mum put in a call when I made 50, he still wouldn't turn it on. He was about five minutes from home at the top of the valley when Mum rang again to tell him that I was on 96. And this time, he relented, so he and Louise heard me get the hundred.

■◀▮▶■

That one innings turned around my career. It was like I'd been ordering drinks at the Last-Chance Saloon on credit and then *bang!* I'd won the lottery. Not only was the tab cleared, but I'd been relocated to the VIP Room where the stool had a cushion on it and your glass was always full. I told the media afterwards that I was thrilled but was also sorry for disappointing so many people over the years. That apology was in some ways directed at me as well, because if the fans were frustrated, it was only a fraction of what I felt. I think the difference in that 143 was that I wasn't fighting myself – I never got to the point where I was satisfied, which meant for once I didn't need to play a rash shot.

The remainder of the World Cup unfolded like a carefully-wrapped birthday present. We built momentum, beat the teams we were supposed to beat and emerged winners from the knock-down, drag-em-out matches that you have to claim if you want to spray the champagne around at the end of it all. It was a magical trip – seeing Andy 'Bic' Bichel produce performances that must have got him very close to the player of the tournament are still among my best cricket memories. Bic's a man after my own heart – he loves his fishing and his rugby league, he's one of the handiest blokes I know, and he's rock-solid on and off the field. His effort to get us past England in the Super Sixes at Port Elizabeth was as good an all-round performance as you're ever likely to see.

I got a few more bats in the tournament, picking up 59 against Namibia and 33 not out against Kenya, but missed out with a duck against the Poms. Things smiled on me again during the semi-final against Sri Lanka in Port Elizabeth, finishing with 91 not out after coming to the crease at 3-51 on a tough, slow and low wicket. I took my time, concentrated on playing straight and addressed each ball on its merits. I had to fight myself when Aravinda de Sliva was bowling his gentle off-breaks and couldn't help thinking: 'How far would I hit this if I was at training?' He knew it too, and was floating them up, hoping I'd lose it. But for once I didn't.

The final was everything you could hope for and we were all over India like a cheap suit from the get-go. I reckon they were terrified that day of losing and showed it by winning the toss and putting us into bat. I mean, why wouldn't they put their batting strength on the board from the outset to put us under pressure chasing? Gilly and Haydos set the scene by smashing the bowlers to all parts of the Bullring before Punter led the way with an extraordinary century, with Damien Martyn showing courage to score 88 painful runs due to a badly broken finger. I was padded up to bat next and sat there for nine overs watching the score mount to 364.

The weather gave us a bit of concern when they started their chase but it stayed true. I picked up a couple of wickets late in the game and when Boof took the final catch, I was that happy, I think my heart stopped for a beat. Bic and I shed a few tears together and I tried to hug as many people as I could get into my arms. After that, it was champagne and cigars – in the dressing room, out in the middle where we poured some beer into the wicket to say thanks, and then back at the hotel. I enjoyed myself, no two ways about it – you don't win a World Cup every day and you certainly don't get the opportunity to re-invent yourself partway through your career every day.

The next morning I got a message that the Gold Coast Dolphins had won the club's inaugural first-grade premiership. How good was that? I let out a big 'woo-hoo' on the team bus because I was that thrilled for the boys, but calling it the best news of the weekend was probably an overstatement, all things considered.

The World Cup was the most incredible thing that has happened to me on a sporting field, and one of the most significant events of my life. Occasionally though, I wonder what would have been if I hadn't made the team, and just where things might have ended up.

CUTTING LOOSE AT THE CUP

2003 ICC WORLD CUP

AUSTRALIA v PAKISTAN
Wanderers Stadium, Johannesburg
11 February 2003 (50-over match)

34.3 Afridi to
Symonds,
FOUR, great
shot through
mid-wicket

● **DEEP SQUARE LEG**

MID-WICKET ●

SQUARE LEG ●

● **FINE LEG**

WICKETKEEPER ●

● **SILLY
MID-C**

● **SLIPS**

● **GULLY**

34.2 Afridi to
Symonds, wide: no
run, way outside off

34.4 Afridi to
Symonds, no run,
Younis fields a
chip shot into the
gully area

● **THIRD MAN**

34.1 Afridi to Symonds,
FOUR, neatly between
slip and gully, both give
chase in vain

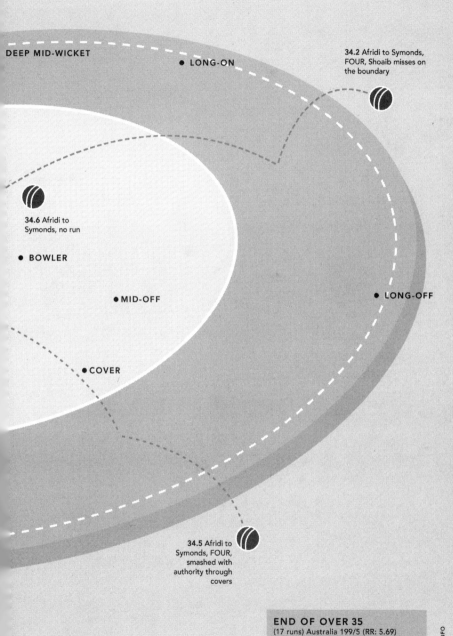

DEEP MID-WICKET

● LONG-ON

34.2 Afridi to Symonds, FOUR, Shoaib misses on the boundary

34.6 Afridi to Symonds, no run

● BOWLER

●MID-OFF

● LONG-OFF

●COVER

34.5 Afridi to Symonds, FOUR, smashed with authority through covers

END OF OVER 35
(17 runs) Australia 199/5 (RR: 5.69)

SHAHID AFRIDI 6-0-41-0 (1w) - Corlett Drive End
A SYMONDS 78* (73b 13x4)
GB HOGG 8* (10b)

IS THIS BROKEN?

By Michael Kasprowicz

About ten years ago, Roy and I were on a long flight to Tasmania, somewhere over Bass Strait. It was back when our coach John Buchanan had been encouraging the players to buy laptops so they could better access the various coaching software packages he was using. I had my laptop out and was checking on some stats when Roy asked me if he could borrow it for a while. Now this was back when I reckon he probably couldn't have found the on/off switch, but he'd heard enough about this 'Internet thing' to know that it might be useful. He told me he was keen to look at some fishing websites and check the tide times for when we got back. I knew where this was going so I handed it over and did my best to keep a straight face when he asked me where he should plug it in. He was most disappointed when he found out that he was unable to access the Internet while 34,000 feet in the air.

Michael says: 'The funny thing is that in the early days, a lot of people were a bit hazy about the Internet and I'm sure Roy wouldn't have been the first person to ask that question on a plane – unfortunately he did it with a bunch of blokes who were just waiting for a slip-up!'

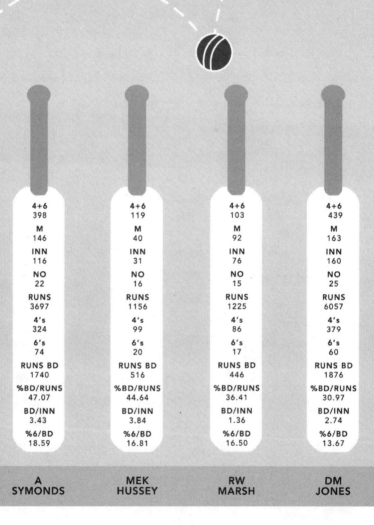

THE MASTER BLASTERS

The percentage of sixes scored in boundaries by Australian One Day International players who have scored more than 100 boundaries

	A SYMONDS	MEK HUSSEY	RW MARSH	DM JONES
4+6	398	119	103	439
M	146	40	92	163
INN	116	31	76	160
NO	22	16	15	25
RUNS	3697	1156	1225	6057
4's	324	99	86	379
6's	74	20	17	60
RUNS BD	1740	516	446	1876
%BD/RUNS	47.07	44.64	36.41	30.97
BD/INN	3.43	3.84	1.36	2.74
%6/BD	18.59	16.81	16.50	13.67

THE MASTER BLASTERS

	RT PONTING	SR WAUGH	AC GILCHRIST	ML HAYDEN
4+6	884	597	1109	466
M	251	325	241	118
INN	245	288	234	114
NO	29	58	9	12
RUNS	9096	7569	8209	4129
4's	768	529	988	416
6's	116	68	121	50
RUNS BD	3768	2524	4678	1964
%BD/RUNS	41.42	33.35	56.99	47.57
BD/INN	3.61	2.07	4.74	4.09
%6/BD	13.12	11.39	10.91	10.73

THE TIN MAN AND THE BAGGY GREEN

When Dorothy finds the wood-chopping Tin Man in the forest in *The Wizard of Oz*, the poor old fella's as stiff and uncoordinated as a 90-year-old cricketer with arthritis – not surprising I suppose after losing a limb and being rebuilt with scrap metal – but as if that weren't enough, he's also in need of a new ticker. I tell this story for a couple of reasons: firstly, when it comes to relationships and matters of the heart, while most of it's been good, some of it's been bad. Very bad. Secondly, those who have had the privilege of seeing me on the dance floor (in other words nearly all of my Queensland and Australian team-mates) reckon the Tin Man and I share a few of the same moves. In fact, according to the very same dressing-room stand-up comics, I must be one of the few people of West Indian heritage on the planet with absolutely no rhythm. It's an argument I won't be having with them, because it's true: I flat-out can't dance. Can't sing either, but that's a whole other story.

Although I've spent quite a bit of time travelling around Asia, the subcontinent and the Caribbean over the years, I've honestly never experienced any 'spiritual' connections with people from that side of my ancestry, at least that I'm aware of. If you'd seen me on my first trip to the West Indies back in 2003, the expression 'fish out of water' would have sprung to mind. There was plenty of laughter from the boys as locals came up and greeted me as 'brother', giving me 'much respect', slapping skin on skin and doing funky stuff with the handshakes. I had nothing: 'Er yeah. G'day mate, pleased to meet ya.' As Chippin often says, I may look like Linford Christie but I sound like Paul Hogan.

Having said this, I'm particularly fond of the West Indian people – especially the cricketers – and as I've mentioned, two of my childhood heroes were Viv Richards and Richie Richardson. I had the thrill of playing against Richie in my first year in England and have been lucky enough to hang out with Viv on a few occasions, most recently in 2003. Viv's a larger-than-life character and even now it *feels* as if he's still 'the man'. People have called me a 'Master Blaster' on the odd occasion, but as far as I'm concerned, I don't come close: Viv is the original and the best. Believe it or not, we haven't talked cricket in any great depth when we've met, but I'd love to sit down properly with him over a beer (or a rum punch) one of these days and listen to all the war stories. He's still a hero of mine, which may sound funny coming from a bloke who's getting into his 30s, but we all need people we can look up to and admire, no matter what our age.

Playing in the Caribbean is an eye-opening experience – and not just because of the cricketing competition. When you walk onto the ground the first thing you hear are the steel drums belting away and the reggae blaring out; this is immediately followed by the roar of the crowd. The locals are drinking their rum punch and it feels like a carnival – in every corner there's something colourful or just plain bizarre going down. As the day wears on, you often catch a waft of ganja smoke on the breeze – I call it 'the blue mist' – it's probably one of the reasons the spectators always seem to be having so much fun!

As a team, we get on really well with the Windies, even if blokes like Tino Best talk at 90 to the dozen and no one has any idea what he's saying. I usually just hand him a beer and laugh along. On their last Australian tour in 2005/06, I tried to lure Brian Lara away from Brisbane for a spell at my local watering hole, but even though he wavered, he put the team first and politely declined. Good on him – the locals might have loved us to death if we'd popped in for a session!

I'm as surprised as anyone at the Windies' form the past few seasons, especially with the likes of Bennett King in charge. I thought Benny plus the Windies would be a formidable combo once they worked each other out, but the pairing hasn't really produced the results so far. Perhaps it goes in cycles. The team has the talent all right: the young all-rounder Dwayne Smith hits the ball as hard and clean as anyone I've seen, and Benny told me that if he ever gets his brain in gear, he could be deadly. That sounds vaguely familiar so I guess I'll be watching his career closely …

Between Christmas and New Year 2004 I was on duty with the Bulls in Tasmania, and when we heard the news of the Boxing Day tsunami I, along with all my team-mates, was gutted. The natural devastation was unlike anything we'd ever seen in our lifetimes. I really felt for the people of Sri Lanka – along with the West Indies, it's a country I love and one in which I've played many memorable games of cricket.

The images of the ruined city of Galle on Sri Lanka's southwest coast were horrible and hard to get your head around. Galle was a beautiful, picture-postcard sort of place, with the walls of its 400-year-old fort encircling the cricket ground, but to see a wrecked bus sitting in the middle of the pitch where we'd celebrated Warney's 500th Test wicket just a few months earlier put our triumph into stark perspective.

The Bulls felt we had to do something to help, so not long after we got back to Brisbane, we joined forces with Rotary International, Australia Post and Brisbane radio station B105 and held a tsunami fund-raiser at Queensland Cricket HQ. The idea was that people who felt like contributing could donate tinned food, blankets, tools, tents and anything else that might be useful. Happily, the response was overwhelming and we collected nearly three tons worth of goods. It turned into a massive day, with everyone pitching in to fill the Australia Post trucks and take the material to a temporary facility at the Brisbane Exhibition Ground. From there, it was sorted and packed into shipping containers bound for the collection various points, where Rotary had contacts ready and waiting to distribute it.

I was really glad that some of the aid was going to Sri Lanka because they were one of the countries hardest hit, and because my memories of playing there were nothing but happy. I'd toured there in February 2004 and was hoping and praying my performances in the ODIs would earn me a run in the Test line-up later in the season. Ultimately, I knew my selection would come down to my efforts in the coloured clothes rather than the whites of the Pura Cup. At that stage, I hadn't scored nearly enough first-class runs with the Bulls to convince anyone I was Test-match material and, as it turned out, it was my bowling – especially the off-spinners – which got me closest to donning a baggy green. In the end, I had a decent ODI series – which Australia won 3-2 – and found that I hadn't lost the secret batting ingredient I'd discovered at the World Cup. Dare I say it, I was almost consistent. Who'd have thought? My cause was helped in the three-day practice game we had between the one-dayers and the start of the Test series where I managed 45 not out and 119 not out in our second innings.

Brooke was with me in Sri Lanka at the time which was great, and I knew Mum and Dad were hanging to come over too, so at the team meeting the night before the first day's play, I quietly asked Punter whether he could give me a heads-up as to the likelihood of my selection. This was something it seemed I'd been waiting all my life to hear and I swear I had goosebumps when he whispered that I'd made the cut! It was another dream come true, but one that could so easily have gone the other way and in the past almost always had. Someone or something must have been looking out for me that day.

AB was the selector on duty and he had both the unenviable task of telling Simon Katich he wasn't in the team and the pleasant job of presenting me with my very first Australia cap. I couldn't have asked for a better way to begin my Test career: AB had been a team-mate and a mentor and when he handed the cap over I think even he was a bit nervous, which just goes to show how much significance we all place in the little green furry thing. The cap is quite hard and

AB was the selector on duty and he had both the unenviable task of telling Simon Katich he wasn't in the team and the pleasant job of presenting me with my very first Australia cap.

firm across your forehead when you first put it on, but you mould it and shape it as you go, although I reckon a buzz cut's got to make things easier than dreads. It doesn't matter though – even if you had no head or the cap was lined with barbed-wire, you'd still wear it and make it fit. When I phoned Mum and Dad they were over the moon and literally jumped on the next plane bound for Colombo.

The morning of the match, I went through my routine, trying in vain to convince myself that it was just like preparing for any other first-class game. Yeah, right. With my baggy green jammed proudly on my head, I attempted to calm my nerves and so I got the white zinc out and did my lips, which is one of the last things I do before I go onto the field. I started using white zinc when I was a kid in Queensland – most of the other kids wore the bronze stuff but Mum hated it because it stained my cricket whites – so I stuck with the white. I'd seen the black and white minstrels but had never thought of myself like that – it was just something I did for practical reasons which soon became a habit and I guess a bit of a trademark. I now put sunscreen on first and then put the zinc over that – it's good protection from the sun, wind, even moonlight! I'm sometimes asked why I wear it at night and the reason is that I feel naked without it on. I actually feel like I've forgotten to do something if I'm not wearing it. I think you'll find most sportsmen and -women have a routine they do before going out to compete.

Sneaking a peak out in the middle of the ground, it was clear it was going to be a 'spinny' pitch, as I like to say, and given that Warney and Murali were both in the race for their 500th Test wicket, it was a sure bet the poor old batsmen weren't going to get off lightly. In my case that turned out to be all too true – I lasted only 15 balls without scoring before Murali made me one of his six first-innings scalps (much to his delight I might add). On the other side of the fence, I did manage to claim my maiden Test scalp (Haydos latched onto a squirt through point from Mahela Jayawardene) while Warney took a sensational five wickets.

The Australian second innings was a mighty effort as Haydos, Damien Martyn and Boof all scored centuries, with Boof's knock an especially emotional one as he'd only recently lost his good mate David Hookes. Chasing 352, the Sri Lankans collapsed in their second innings with Warney and Stuart MacGill taking nine of the ten wickets to fall, giving Warney a whopping ten for the match, including his 500th. He reached the milestone when Hashan Tillakaratne went to sweep, only to get a top edge, sending the ball straight up into the air to where I was fielding at short mid-wicket. It was a textbook catch but I've learned the hard way that no catch is as simple as it looks. Sometimes the seemingly straightforward ones are the hardest to take because you have time to think. I wasn't taking any chances this time and I crushed the ball so tightly it nearly popped back out. Warney was pretty chuffed, as we all were, and it gave us just the start to the series that we needed. The celebrations after the win were enthusiastic to say the least, and there are a few photos floating around of a mob of us (including AB) up on the walls of the Fort shirtless and singing 'Under The Southern Cross I Stand' …

Mum and Dad were tickled pink with pride, and I hope they felt that all of the sacrifices they'd made since picking me up out of the crib at my foster mother's place were worth it. I know I did. I was stoked that Brooke had been there too. We'd been through a fair bit over the years and it was fitting she was able to share in the moment.

Actually, Brooke was a bit of a local celebrity, with the cameras regularly crossing to her sitting with Mum and Dad in the stands. After a while, everyone knew who she was and she became famous around Galle – the locals called her 'Miss Brooke' whenever we went to the shops and although she thought it was a wind-up, I genuinely had nothing to do with it …

I was retained for the Second Test in Kandy but didn't quite nail it with either the bat or the ball and was overlooked for the final Test in Colombo. I was disappointed, but not devastated. I'd had a taste of glory and wanted more, but I realised that earning a Test spot and retaining it were two mighty challenges that rarely went hand in hand.

I had a contract to go back to Kent in England following the Sri Lankan tour, but before that, there was the small matter of a wedding to consider …

I've only twice seriously thought about giving up cricket: the first time was back in 2002 when I considered trying my hand at rugby league, and the second was just before the 2005 Ashes tour. It's not something a lot of people know about, and I find it difficult to talk about it even now, but how I came to be in that spot goes back almost 13 years.

I'd known Brooke Marshall since starting at All Saints high school – she was this beautiful, outgoing blonde with the most dazzling smile – but things only got serious during my last year there in 1993 when Brooke was in Year 11. By the time I left for my first long overseas playing stint in 1995, we'd been in a steady relationship for almost three years. With our various commitments, particularly my sporting ones, we'd had to make the best of the

I've only twice seriously thought about giving up cricket: the first time was back in 2002 when I considered trying my hand at rugby league, and the second was just before the 2005 Ashes tour.

sometimes lengthy periods apart, but inevitably, even if we'd split up for a while, we always came back to one another. We were in love, and when we weren't together I'd be wondering how she was and what she was doing; I think there's some truth to the old saying that absence makes the heart grow fonder. In those days we had a sort of magnetic attraction for each other, and when things were good, they were great. Of course the opposite usually applies and I look back now and know that I must have tested her patience big time.

By 2003 I'd been playing and touring relentlessly for almost a decade and I think it's fair to say that the lifestyle had taken its toll on our relationship. I was in England during my second last season with Kent, and by the time I was due to come back to Australia, Brooke and I had been apart for nearly six months. I couldn't stop wondering where things were going and whether or not we'd be able to make a future together. I came to the conclusion that I couldn't and shouldn't go any further knowing that I hadn't given the relationship my best shot. At the time I was sure I didn't want to be with anyone else and so I decided that it was now or never.

I'd bought a beautiful diamond in South Africa on the 2000 tour, but like a lot of blokes, the whole commitment thing freaked me out and so the rock had just been gathering dust in the bottom drawer. I hadn't got it made into a ring because I didn't know what style Brooke would like; I had a vague idea of course but as it was a wedding ring, I didn't think it was right to make that sort of decision without her input. To be honest, I was also scared at the prospect of going down on bended knee, pulling out the velvet box, popping the question and then getting a big fat 'no'! It was by no means a done deal and I knew that between the touring, the travelling and me just being me, I'd put Brooke through the wringer more than once.

Anyway, as soon as I got home I steeled myself and called her. We arranged to meet at the Norman Hotel at Woolloongabba; we could have a drink, maybe a bite to eat and good old catch up. I put the diamond in a black velvet-lined ring box and jumped in the ute. On the way I bought a huge bunch of flowers and laid them on the passenger seat, but when I pulled into the car park at the Norman I froze and couldn't move. It was worse than going out to bat in a big game – not even in the same league. I was paralysed by a combination of old-fashioned nerves and fear of rejection. But there was no going back and if I got shot down in flames, then so be it, at least I wouldn't die wondering 'what if?'.

I was sitting there with sweaty palms, heart thudding in my chest, unable to move, churning through what I was about to say, when I saw Brooke's car pull into the car park. She got out, came around to the ute's passenger-side door, opened it and straightaway saw the flowers sitting on the passenger seat.

'Wow, who are you going to see?' she said.

'Someone special.'

'Well, they're lucky, aren't they?' She then started chit chatting as though nothing unusual was about to happen, suggesting we go inside instead of sitting in the car park. In her defence, she wasn't a mind reader, so how could she have known?

I could barely contain myself. 'Just before we do that,' I began, 'there's something I need to ask you.' Hands shaking, I reached down to get the ring box. 'Brooke, I wanted to ask if you'd marry me –' I opened the black velvet box, but there was nothing inside – the diamond had gone! It must have fallen out and for a second, I thought I'd have to continue with an empty velvet box.

But there it was, sitting on a towel I had on the front seat, so I grabbed it, put it back and handed it over. It was all a bit teary for a while then, before Brooke pulled us together and insisted we go inside and have a drink, calm down and work out what was going to happen. She hadn't said no, hadn't said yes, only that she'd have to think about it. I thought I was still in with a pretty good chance.

◀▮▶

I waited about a week for an answer. The Dolphins were playing a one-dayer in Toowoomba on the Sunday and we were bussing it up after our premiership match on the Saturday. Brooke rang just after we'd left so I got off the bus and waited for her by the highway. When we got to the hotel where we were staying, she said, 'I've had a good think and I've spoken to some people about what you said. Ask me again.'

It had been a long day, what with playing cricket and driving up the Toowoomba range, but I couldn't miss the chance. 'Ask you *what* again?'

'You know – ask me again!'

'That's a bit unfair. I've already asked you once.'

She was smiling but insistent. 'Ask me again.'

I couldn't keep up the charade so I got down on one knee and asked her to marry me.

This time she said yes and I was as happy as this bloke they call Larry.

There was a bit to organise and we checked the cricket calendar and tried to find a window in the next six months. April 2004 looked good, and as it happened, we were able to be in Sri Lanka together for my Test debut before coming home for the wedding. It was a beautiful day – I don't think I'd seen Brooke happier and it goes without saying that I had the just about the biggest split watermelon grin you've ever seen. We were married in St John's Cathedral by the Reverend Canon Len Nairn, who'd taught us at All Saints, and had our reception down near the Brisbane River at Stamford Plaza. It was a bit of a who's who of cricketers: Buck, Haydos and Gilly among the guests, and Mahbo doing the honours as Master of Ceremonies. Everyone had plenty to laugh about that night with Mahbo and Motty on the microphone. I even broke my golden rule and danced in public.

The future was bright: I was newly married to my childhood sweetheart, my cricket was on the up, I was still fit and young (well, at least I *felt* young), so what could possibly go wrong?

<hr/>

This book has given me an invaluable opportunity to reflect on my career and my life to this point: on balance I've been incredibly lucky and I think I've made more right decisions than wrong ones, but from time to time I've sailed too close to the wind and have made some woeful mistakes. 2004 may have begun brightly, but it ended in darkness. If this was *Judge Judy*, I'd probably be expected to break down and confess all at this point, but that's not my style. I owe it to Brooke to be honest, but I'm also firm that everyone is entitled to a private life, even those of us who are frequently in the public eye. All

I want to say is that my actions damaged our relationship and if I had my time over I know I'd do things differently – whether that would have changed how things ended up, I can't be sure.

Our friends in England and Australia were a huge support to us both when our brand new marriage came unstuck. In particular, I was lucky to be able to rely on Joe Dawes and Mahbo for help when I got back to Australia in early September 2004. I lived with Joey briefly and then moved in with Mahbo and his wife Debbie for several weeks, and did my best to repay their hospitality by being an on-call breakfast-maker and DVD-changer for their kids Lily and Christopher. Mahbo and I had many all-night sessions drinking coffee and talking it through. You know when you stuff something up and you find yourself wishing you could turn back the clock? All you do is run through those 'what ifs' in your head, but it changes precisely nothing.

Mahbo was brilliant, but I realised I was well out of my depth and so I went to see Phil Jauncey, the psychologist who works with the Australian Cricket team, the Bulls, Brisbane Lions and the Brisbane Broncos, and asked him how I should handle things. Some weeks I'd speak with him twice a day. It was stressful for everyone involved – I'm sure I wasn't the best company during this period and

You know when you stuff something up and you find yourself wishing you could turn back the clock? All you do is run through those 'what ifs' in your head, but it changes precisely nothing.

I know I lost a lot of weight and had trouble coping with everyday things. I didn't feel like playing cricket because I was in such an emotional mess, but I'd kit up and do my best; it turned out that these were often the times when I just let my instincts take over and ended up playing really well. I may have looked focused and in control out in the middle, but on the inside I was confused, angry and ashamed, endlessly mulling over how or if I could save my marriage.

In late September 2004 I scored a hundred in a One Day International Champions Trophy match against Pakistan at Lords. Brooke had come to England and we were talking, doing our best to work out whether there was a way forward. On the day I scored that century at Lords, she was in the stands watching, and it meant the world to me. Even from out in the middle, and in spite of everything that had happened that year, I could see her smiling. That innings was for her. I told myself that maybe someone had been looking down on us and had decided that a brief moment of happiness was okay.

Brooke came to an ING Cup game late in the 2004/05 season – I remember seeing her arrive and again it lifted my spirits no end – as well as the Pura Cup final against NSW in March 2005 at the Gabba. That game wasn't nearly as much fun as the one at Lords – in the end we lost a cliffhanger by a single wicket. We were bloody disappointed: Mahbo was in tears on the field afterwards and I kept thinking to myself, 'All up, this has been one ordinary season.'

That loss brought Brooke and I back together for a time and we reached a point where we both thought we might be able to give it another go. I guess the last thing we needed was for me to get on a plane and fly to England for the 2005 Ashes tour. Even though it's one of the pinnacles of the game, I seriously thought about stepping down from it, and cricket altogether. My reasoning was that if there was any chance of rebuilding my marriage, then perhaps I was better off without cricket. I spoke at length with Brooke and Phil Jauncey and Phil said that while giving up cricket would have shown commitment, I needed to ask myself whether I was prepared to lose the two things I loved, because if things didn't work out with Brooke, I'd have nothing.

I decided that if we were going to make the most of a second chance, then it would have to involve cricket, because that was one of the few things I could rely upon to give us a future. I signed a deal with Lancashire prior to the start of the one-dayers and Brooke and I agreed to give it another go. Perhaps that was the wrong decision, perhaps it wouldn't have mattered what we tried … but that was the path we chose.

Brooke came to England and we did our best, though I can't say it was smooth sailing – there were times when I was drinking too much when I thought I was just having a few to unwind – but we were trying and that was the main thing. Throughout, the boys were

I spoke at length with Brooke and Phil Jauncey and Phil said that while giving up cricket would have shown commitment, I needed to ask myself whether I was prepared to lose the two things I loved, because if things didn't work out with Brooke, I'd have nothing.

very supportive and I kept telling myself that if we just hung in there, we'd be right. Again, in hindsight, returning to play in England was probably the wrong decision. The life of a County cricketer doesn't allow for much downtime and with both of us away from our friends and families back in Australia, there just wasn't the support network you need when times are tough.

As you've probably gathered by now, our story didn't have a fairytale ending, and in mid-September 2005 Brooke decided to call it quits and return to Australia. She left me a letter explaining why she was going home, and a white pebble. She'd been to Bali earlier in the year and had picked up two rocks from one of the beaches – a black one and a white one. I had feared this was how it would pan out but I still didn't expect it to come to such a sudden end. I was a mess and was late for the game the next day as I tried to sort myself out and come to grips with what had happened. My world had been turned inside out, and after almost 13 years, it was going to take a long time to accept that Brooke was no longer going to be a part of it.

◄█▮█►

I came home too a few weeks later and tried to get back into some sort of routine. One evening I was out fishing by myself on the seaway near South Stradbroke Island. I'd been filleting a few fish that I'd caught – it was really messy work – and as I shook the slime and blood from my left hand, my wedding ring slid off my finger and went over the side and into the ocean. I froze and felt physically ill for a moment. In a panic, I immediately rang Brooke: she did her best to settle me and, as I recall, handled it a lot better than I did. I'm not really superstitious, but I reckon even the most hardheaded cynic would've had trouble dismissing the significance of this.

More than a year has passed and I now accept what's done is done. I'm sorry Brooke had to deal with what she did and as I say if I had my time again I'd do things differently, but I believe you learn from your mistakes even more than your successes, and I know I've emerged from the whole experience a changed person. Of course nothing can alter the past, but when it comes to the future, I'm confident of two things: I reckon I can handle pretty much whatever life has to throw at me, and I'm going to try with all my heart to stick to that yellow brick road.

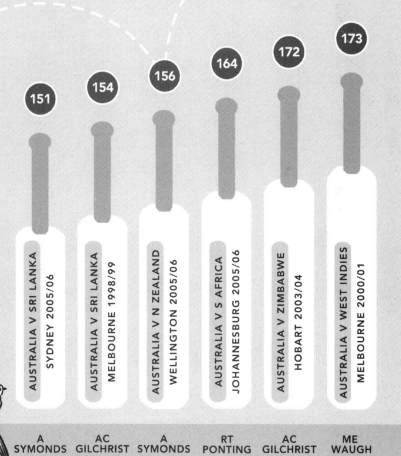

HIGHEST SCORES IN ONE DAY INTERNATIONAL CRICKET

By Australians

151 — AUSTRALIA V SRI LANKA, SYDNEY 2005/06 — A SYMONDS

154 — AUSTRALIA V SRI LANKA, MELBOURNE 1998/99 — AC GILCHRIST

156 — AUSTRALIA V N ZEALAND, WELLINGTON 2005/06 — A SYMONDS

164 — AUSTRALIA V S AFRICA, JOHANNESBURG 2005/06 — RT PONTING

172 — AUSTRALIA V ZIMBABWE, HOBART 2003/04 — AC GILCHRIST

173 — AUSTRALIA V WEST INDIES, MELBOURNE 2000/01 — ME WAUGH

CHAPTER 14

CARDIFF

I didn't feel the first bottle of water that Michael 'Pup' Clarke poured over me. Didn't feel the second one either for that matter. In fact the only water that finally registered was when I was standing up, albeit unsteadily, in the shower. It was weird – I'd put my head down for a few minutes and had dropped off into a deep sleep. Kept my boots on, jeans too. In fact, I kept on everything I'd been wearing the night before. Now I was drenched and Pup was doing his frantic best to get me on the bus …

It all started harmlessly enough. Isn't it always the way? We were in Wales, staying in the beautiful capital, Cardiff, and with team-mate Shane Watson going through a bit of a rough patch after a relationship break-up, and me nursing my own inner turmoil, we thought we'd unwind over a few bevies. We were taking on Bangladesh the next day in a One Day International at Sophia Gardens. I generally hit the sack around 10.30 pm before a day game and no later than midnight for a day/nighter. I don't have a lot of problems with nerves and the like and, as those who have toured with me know, I'm a world-class sleeper.

I realise now I made my first mistake that night well before I left the hotel. 'Ah, it's only Bangladesh ... a bit of fizz won't be a worry and it'll be good for Watto,' was what I told myself as I headed off to dinner, in some ways giving myself an out before I had even got the first drink in my hands.

Dinner came and went and we got ourselves nice and comfortable in the Walkabout Pub. I was aware of a few of the guys leaving and then the clock chimed midnight and all of a sudden I was in choppy water. Pup had an inkling that I wasn't following the usual routine because he took my room key off me before he left. There's a bit of an unwritten rule on tour: 'until midnight' is your time but 'after midnight' is team time. I've subsequently pieced together a bit of what happened and obviously I was in a very happy frame of mind and looking for others to share it with. There were plenty of other pubs within walking distance of the Walkabout and I reckon I had a look, and a bit more, in most of them. They were what we call 'crab pots' – easy to enter with something attractive waiting inside, but very difficult to get out of. Barney claims I swore I kicked on with 'the republican' of the Walkabout after they shut down for the night. But I don't remember saying that, although I'm hardly an authority.

Anyone reading this book who's found themselves still going as the sky begins to lighten will know that time seems to accelerate. And so it was that I ended up back in the foyer of the team hotel with the light being a lot more natural than artificial. I made it to my room without any problems but had to go back down to the foyer for the spare key because Pup of course had taken mine. And that's when I smelled the bacon and eggs coming from the buffet and decided a decent feed was in order.

About eight eggs and a dozen rashers of bacon later, I noticed a few early birds straggling in – company I rarely keep. Buck looked surprised to see me but didn't pop over for a brekky chat, fortunately or unfortunately as it turned out. I made as discreet an exit as I could, (semi) aware that jeans, going-out shirt and boots were not usual breakfast attire.

Then I fell asleep and the next thing I know I'm being pinched, prodded and poked before getting drenched with water. With Pup's help I got onto the bus but it's fair to say that I probably didn't keep the low profile that he'd had urged me to keep and by the time we reached the ground, questions were being asked. Another shower didn't help and when the warm-up started on field, the jig was pretty well up, especially when I slipped off the wheelie bin that I was doing my stretches against.

Punter came over and asked me straight out what time I got in.

I thought I might be able to brazen it out with him and said, 'About 2.30 am.'

He fired back, 'Are you still pissed?'

I told him no, I was right. But he'd heard enough. Buck came over and asked me what was going on.

'Nothing,' I replied, trying not to breathe on him.

'That's not what the captain says. Have you been drinking?'

'Nah … ah well, not much,' I replied, my resolve to hang tough shot to pieces.

'You're drunk. You're not playing today.'

Once more I thought I could pull it back. 'No, I'm right to go. I'm playing.'

It takes a lot to get Buck cranky but I had his number that day. 'No, Roy, you're not playing and you'd better sort yourself out.' With that he turned and stormed off. Then Gilly came over and he was ropeable as well.

I knew then I was for the high jump but part of me kept thinking I could ride it out. I was kidding myself of course. There was some discussion among the boys that an injury or flu should be used as the excuse for my absence and as it started to sink in that I was gone, I fired up. 'If you're going drop me, then you better tell them why or I will.' I was now showering myself in petrol and standing on a woodpile playing with matches. In hindsight, I don't know why I was even disputing it. I was in more strife than the early settlers and should have copped everything they threw at me.

Cracker Hohns was at dinner in Fortitude Valley in Brisbane that night when he got the phone call from Cricket Australia. The Valley is a cosmopolitan place but there still would have been some startled fellow diners when he expressed the depth of his anger. He's told me since that had it been up to him, there would have been no discussion – I would have been sent home on the next flight departing London.

That day was a shocker. I sat by myself, with very few people speaking to me, knowing full well I was in disgrace. I did what I could to stay involved, and ran the drinks a few times, but it was a miserable few hours. I was tired and would have given anything to have a quick kip, but there was no way I was going to succumb – that would've just added insult to injury. Compounding the embarrassment was the fact that the Bangladeshis chose that precise day to plant one right on the chin of the Aussie team to continue a miserable start to the Ashes tour.

After the game, we got behind closed doors and my hearing under the internal team system that was instituted to deal with 'Spirit of Cricket' issues got underway. There wasn't any real fight left in me by then. I knew I'd stuffed up big time. Pup stood up for me when the talk turned to additional penalties and said that I had already received a harsh punishment in being dropped from the team. He also told the group how disappointed he was in himself that he hadn't stepped in to head me off at the pass before I hit trouble. I was glad to have his voice in my corner but I knew that I had done the crime and had to accept the time. He's told me since that he spoke up because he felt partly responsible as he knew I was going through a tough patch in my personal life and probably hadn't tried hard enough to get me to come home. Based on the snippets I remember, he wouldn't have had a snowball's chance in hell.

The team meeting went for ages and as a group, the disappointment they felt in my actions meant this wasn't going to blow over with a slap on the wrist and a 'naughty boy Roy' speech. They might have been my mates but they were united in their fury at my actions. In the end they handed down what was an appropriate penalty – I was suspended for the next ODI against England in Bristol the following day and fined my match fee for both games. I

The team meeting went for ages and as a group, the disappointment they felt in my actions meant this wasn't going to blow over with a slap on the wrist and a 'naughty boy Roy' speech.

was also told in the clearest possible terms that any further misdemeanours would see me sent packing. For good.

Looking back, my embarrassment and regret are stronger than ever. I said afterwards that I felt as if my guts had been ripped out because I'd let down some of my closest mates, my family and, let's face it, the whole country. That hasn't changed. I can't apologise to everyone but if I could, I would.

＝｜｜＝

My suspension over, I was determined to salvage something from the series. As it turned out, things fell into place. The next two games saw me score 73 off 81 balls to help us beat England by 57 runs in a day/nighter at Chester-le-Street and then pick up career-best ODI bowling figures against Bangladesh in Manchester as Australia took revenge for the Cardiff loss with a ten-wicket win. The wicket gripped a fair bit that day and my 5-18 from 7.2 overs was one of those times when it was handy to be able to bowl a bit of spin.

Things stayed on the up for the rest of the Nat-West triangular series and the Nat-West Challenge against England before the Ashes battle got underway in earnest. I picked up 74 off 75 balls against England in the game that finished as a no-result due to rain and was able to contribute a few runs (29) and a run-out of Paul Collingwood for 53 in the final.

The end of the one-day series meant a return to English County cricket – on this occasion, Lancashire, a great side with a wealth of talent, including my old Queensland team-mate Stuart Law, as well as Freddie Flintoff and Muttiah Muralitharan. It was a fair end to an otherwise disastrous season.

Back home, in the lead-up to the ICC's matches between Australia and the Rest of the World in Melbourne in October 2005, the question arose as to whether I'd be eligible for any awards at the Allan Border Medal presentation later in the season. I knew what I thought was the right thing to do but I wanted to take it to the team. They were split about 50-50, but I didn't want to be standing up to accept an award if any of my team-mates thought I shouldn't be getting it, so I told the boys I'd rule myself ineligible to avoid any potential hassles. In hindsight, my stance came back to bite me at the Medal presentation night. From the outset, everyone seemed to have a line about me getting on the drink. I expected a few cracks, and I'm usually the first bloke to laugh at myself, but it was relentless and I got a bit annoyed, especially as there was plenty of celebration of the drinking feats of previous eras going on.

In the end, I polled enough votes to be in a three-way tie for the One Day International player of the year award, and based on the countback system normally employed, would have won it for the second year in a row. But as I'd ruled myself ineligible that wasn't to be, with Mike Hussey continuing his outstanding start to his international career by collecting the gong. A number of people on the night were under the impression that Cricket Australia had ruled me out, so I was secretly pleased that Punter spoke up about me afterwards, if only to confirm in my own mind that my stuff-up in Cardiff hadn't irreparably damaged our relationship.

During the 2005/06 series against the West Indies, I asked Brian Lara to sign a shirt for me. I'm not a big collector of memorabilia – I've got a few stumps and a few bats – but I don't mind swapping and signing shirts with blokes I've played against. Apparently Sachin Tendulkar has got one of mine in a bar-restaurant he owns, (I signed it 'The man we all want to be') and I was lucky enough to get one in return from him with the message: 'We all want to hit the ball as hard as you.' I've also been fortunate to swap shirts with Wasim Akram and Murali, each of them personalised in some way. But Brian Lara's message is easily the shortest and most memorable. It simply reads:

'Roy, I loved Cardiff too.'

Great cricketer and a funny, funny man.

MOST SIXES IN ONE DAY INTERNATIONALS

By Australians

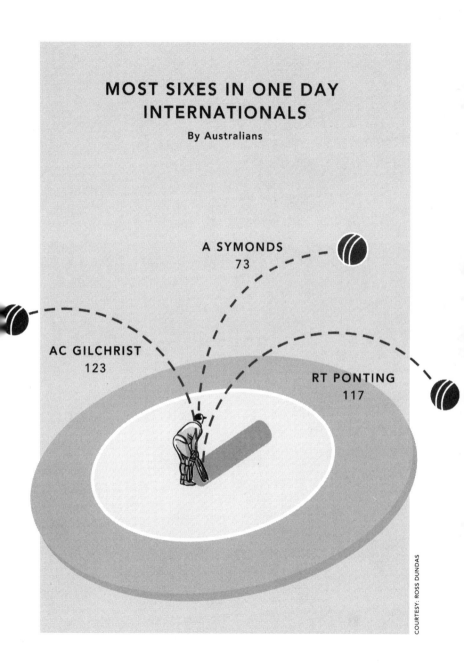

A SYMONDS
73

AC GILCHRIST
123

RT PONTING
117

ROY'S DRESSING-ROOM SLIPS

By a number of team-mates

'Kasper, when's the RSPCA date of your wedding again?'

'What's that movie with Jerry Maguire in it called again?'

'What's your mother's maiden name, Roy?'

'It's Barbara.'

Using the trivia under the caps of XXXX GOLD stubbies to pass the time after play ...

Questioner: 'What sort of animal is a bushmaster?' *Correct answer: A type of snake.*

Roy: 'I know this one – it's a type of BBQ.' *Much laughter ensues.* 'No wait, that's a *Beefmaster*.'

CHAPTER 15

PINK GALAHS
MIGHT FLY

The Wolverine, All-Aussie Adventurer Russell Coight and Galleries of Pink Galahs – got to be one of the most unlikely combinations for anyone to call upon to lift them to a career high. But they worked for me when I was down a hole and wondering how to get out. So how did actor Hugh Jackman, comedian Glenn Robbins and singer John Williamson club together to assist cricketer Andrew Symonds? Well, they didn't gather round for a 'Let's Help Roy' telethon or anything like that, but each of them, in their own way, gave me a boost around the 2005 Boxing Day Test, a match where I found my Test career hanging by a thread.

Year in, year out, the Boxing Day Test is the biggest cricket event in Australia, and walking out onto the MCG before a packed house is a special moment that very few people get to experience. If you'd said to me that I would be in that position at the start of the 2005/06 season, you wouldn't have been able to wipe the smile off my dial. But by the time Christmas Day came around, I honestly didn't want to open my present of a baggy green on Boxing Day at the 'G'. The writing was on the wall in big bold letters that unless I came up with something extraordinary against South Africa, I'd pretty well done my dash as far as Test cricket was concerned.

I'd donned the Australia cap for just the third time ever, and the first time on Australian soil, for the second Test against the West Indies in Hobart in November. This came in the wake of Shane 'Watto' Watson's unlucky dive on the final day of the first Test at the Gabba that resulted in a serious shoulder injury. I managed to hit 163 against South Australia in Adelaide the day after Watto went down, which turned out to be rather timely. Even though Watto and I are different types of all-rounders, the selectors called upon me to fill the role for the second Test at Bellerive Oval. I'd been honoured to make my debut for Australia in Sri Lanka in 2004 but there was a special thrill at the prospect of wearing the baggy green on my home turf. In the end, there wasn't much to write home about from Hobart – I scored just the one run and returned 0-17 – but with Australia winning by nine wickets, I was retained for the next Test in Adelaide.

The Adelaide Oval has been a happy hunting ground in the past for me but I didn't come up with a bag full in this Test either. Chatting about the knock with Haydos afterwards, he reckoned my very

Making the grade in Tests is one of the toughest things to achieve as a player, and I was probably guilty of trying to approach the game in a manner that was unnatural.

patient nine runs off 51 balls had been the perfect way to start an innings … if I had been him. Unfortunately, in trying to 'play' like a Test cricketer, I had gone right away from the things that worked for me in first-class and one-day cricket. Making the grade in Tests is one of the toughest things to achieve as a player, and I was probably guilty of trying to approach the game in a manner that was unnatural.

Haydos has said, and I agree with him, that a batsman's pass mark in Test cricket is 50. If you get 30 or 40, you might as well have got a duck because it provides the same level of assistance to the team. Teams are rewarded by players who score 100s and 200s, and that requires large doses of patience, courage and self-belief. The other thing I noticed was One Day International success meant little when it came to the Tests. The sheer amount of time involved was one of the biggest obstacles to overcome. You can control the pacing of a one-day game to a degree, but with a Test, the time is as big a challenge as facing the new ball.

I finished the Adelaide Test in a winning team but also with more than a few pundits questioning my spot, especially with Pup spanking a double century for NSW against Queensland in the Pura Cup after being dropped from the Australian team.

With the three Tests against the West Indies completed, the next opponents in March 2006 were a South African team that was expected to provide us with a tight tussle in what would be six Tests in a row, three in Australia and three in South Africa in March 2006. But before we could get to grips with the Proteas, we were on a plane to New Zealand for three one-dayers against the Kiwis for the Chappell-Hadlee Trophy in early December.

I don't know whether it was the change of colour, but pulling on the yellow one-day strip was like donning a favourite pair of jeans after a tough day at the office in a suit and tie. It had the desired effect on me as a player, with our second game against the Black Caps in Wellington giving me one of those rare moments when everything that could go right, did. The scorebook records a score of 156 off 127 balls, with the footnote being four sixes in an over off Chris Cairns as Australia piled on 5-322, with Pup (82) and me putting on a big partnership. It was easily the freest I had felt playing in an ODI. We had wickets in hand, men to burn and a feeling of absolute, complete freedom. I had no care for my wicket and there was no thought of self-preservation. Rather, it was just 'hit the ball as far as I can, every time'. I didn't target Chris intentionally, although as one of their key players, it helped our cause to knock him out of the attack. He's done the same sort of thing himself and as an all-rounder, there's always a bit of 'live by the sword, die by the sword' involved. Some days you get bitten, some days you do the biting.

◼‖▶

I was picked for the First Test against South Africa in Perth in December, putting 13 and 25 on the board and rolling my arm for just one over. My form was again patchy going into Boxing Day and frankly, I knew I hadn't done enough to hold onto my spot. And that's where Test cricket can mess with your mind, because you find yourself worrying about holding down your selection first, rather than looking to continue the sort of performances that got you picked in the first place. It's hard not to think like that because you want to be in the team so badly and it's not until you score X amount of runs or take Y number of wickets that you can tell yourself that you *will* be there next match and can look forward to it. Still, the selectors stuck with me for the second Test in Melbourne, even though the nagging little voice inside my head was telling me that this surely must be my last chance.

When you find yourself thinking that way, you need to play to your strengths. I knew Mum and Dad, my grandfather, brother and sister were going to be at the 'G' and that they'd be looking out for me. And as it turned out, there were others out there who wanted to do their bit in giving me a boost. It's easy to lose touch with reality in the Australian team set-up sometimes. You'll be sorting out your pads in your kit and look up to see the Prime Minister walk into the room with a few minders and begin chatting with Gilly, or Russell Crowe pop in to catch up with Warney. You get used to it and sometimes even strike up a bit of a friendship with someone who's visited. I'll confess that having met the PM a few times, I feel confident enough to bend his ear on occasion about the amount of tax that athletes pay! The boys wind me up a bit so when he comes along, I make the point of collaring him. Hasn't had any effect yet though, so maybe I'll have to work on my negotiating skills.

Anyway, a few days before the Test, comedian and massive cricket fan Glenn Robbins, famous for his work in 'Kath and Kim', 'The Panel' and 'Russell Coight's All Aussie Adventures', came by training. I love his character Russell Coight, the hapless Aussie bushman who's forever trying to show off his bushcraft only for things to end in disaster. We had a chat and he cheered me up no end with his best wishes for the Test. Boxing Day morning also produced a nice little pick-me-up when I got to the ground to find a fax from John Williamson. I've been fortunate enough to meet him a few times and his song 'Galleries of Pink Galahs' is one of my all-time favourites. He's a good bloke and I was thrilled to get his best wishes for the Test. He signed it with a little drawing of a gumnut and a gum leaf and I kept re-reading that fax after the opening two days when nothing seemed to work.

I had tried to be positive going into the opening day and quickly found that it meant zilch. The South Africans knew that I was one of the weak spots in the Aussie armour and there was plenty of chirping in the field when I came out to bat. We were in a good position after going in first, but I didn't have the time or opportunity to point that out to the South Africans. One ball later and I was on the way back as Andre Nel celebrated wildly after putting a ball just where I could nick it to the 'keeper. I don't know what the fans were feeling but I know I was sick to the guts.

That evening after play, actor Hugh Jackman dropped by to say g'day. It was the first time I'd seen him in the flesh as opposed to a movie or TV screen and it struck me how full of life and enthusiasm he was, in stark contrast to me at the time. He was moving about the room meeting the boys – he shook hands as much as anyone I've ever seen – but when he got to me, I said something like, 'Sorry, but I won't be that much fun at the moment.'

'Ah, that's okay, mate, I understand,' he said. 'It's not easy what you're going through. Hang in there though. I'm sure you'll get some in the second innings.'

If best wishes counted for anything, I was on track for a big payday.

◼▮▮▶

The next morning, I went over things in my head to see if I could find the key to unlocking the puzzle that would get me some runs. I'd done the extra training, was hitting the ball okay but was just nervous. A bloke who didn't appear to get anxious, at least to me, was Mike Hussey. He came up with a gem of an innings to lift us to 355 and put Australia back on top.

When South Africa went into bat on the third day, I had a few near misses with catches and wasn't entirely sure what was going to come out when Punter tossed me the ball for a spell of bowling. I look at the scorecard now and marvel at the difference a bit of confidence can make. As I've often said, I'd like to face me for a living, and I'm sure the South African batsmen relaxed slightly when they saw me up the other end instead of Glenn McGrath or Brett Lee or Shane Warne. Mark Boucher and Herschelle Gibbs were putting on a solid partnership before I tossed in a big in-swinger that caught Boucher near the stumps. I gave the appeal plenty and was surprised and relieved when the decision went my way. The next over, Gibbs, who on 94 was readying himself for a big ton, left the gate open for me to dip one through and bowl him. After terrorising many a bowler or fielder in my time with a good hair rub, the boys made sure they gave the dreaddies a nice old polish and scrub when they got to me. After watching the replays, I was embarrassed rather than ecstatic after seeing my carry-on. It was some sort of war dance. Who knows where that came from.

It got better though, with Shaun Pollock falling a few overs later, also leg before wicket, to give me 3-15. Again, the adrenaline surge meant my celebrations most probably resembled sheer madness. We finished them off to take a lead of 44 runs into our second innings, where I was able to sit back and have the pleasure of watching 'Matt the Bat' start to turn the screws. Taking those wickets certainly pepped me up and when I spoke to the media after play, I told them that when I batted again in the match, I'd try to hit the first ball I received down the ground for four.

On the morning of day four, I bumped into Ian Chappell at the ground and had a bit of a chat with him about how I was going. After listening, he said, 'Son, it seems to me that you've got to get out there and play some shots.' I went to myself, 'Hmm, sounds reasonable.' The way the game was setting up, we were going to be able to treat it like a one-dayer and that suited me. We wanted to have a bowl and there was going to be the need for quick runs at some point.

Although I'd bowled well, I was never going to make the team on my bowling. As it stood, I'd be packing my bags and calling the taxi to go to the airport at the end of the game. I remember sitting with Gilly as play went on and he was a bit nervous too because there had been talk that he could be dropped because he'd hit a rough patch. We were half-joking among ourselves that this could be our last Test together. We were trying to keep our spirits up too, so I'd hate to think what we would have talked about if we had been really depressed.

Haydos had done all the hard work and so when I got to the crease following the dismissal of Huss, the pressure was off, and I could bat like it was a one-dayer. Haydos was of the same opinion – 'just smash 'em mate' – was his straightforward advice. Instead of facing someone like Makhaya Ntini, who can be a handful for a new batsman, I was staring down at Graeme Smith. He's not the worst bowler in the game by a long shot and the ball he bowled to get Mike Hussey had jumped out of the rough. But even before my first was delivered, I patted the pitch down and said to myself, 'If this is in my slot, I'm going down the track here and am going to smack him.' My hands were shaking but I just had to bite the bullet and take him on. The first two balls weren't in the zone but sure enough, the third was where I wanted it and I walloped him down the ground for six. With the signal dropped, the line was clear and the loco was steaming down the track. Andre Nel was huffing and puffing and carrying on at the other end and when Nicky Boje came into the attack, I went after him as well. Haydos started to do likewise and it was sixes and fours rather than ones and twos. I hit Nel back over his head for six and that brought up 50. I took a moment then, telling myself, 'Oh well, that's not bad.'

I could see the boys were up and cheering. Haydos stood and delivered and got a great hundred. We'd been through a lot and he had been a big part of my cricket evolution. I'd scored about 100 runs from nine innings before that knock and while the 72 didn't cement a spot, it kept me in the side for more Tests than had seemed possible. Santa might have been a bit late that year, but he made sure he delivered an extra-special pressie when he did track me down.

I dead-set floated through the rest of that day as we tried to wrap up the South African innings. Jacques Kallis was still there and, along with Herschelle Gibbs, is one of the batsmen in their line-up who can turn the momentum of a game. Punter tossed me the ball for a few overs and the wave of good fortune I'd been riding picked me up for a last surge into the shore. It was just after the last drinks break when I got one to dip away late from Kallis, who got the edge on the way through to Gilly.

I was that pumped as I charged down the wicket that I just about wiped out Warney. I lifted him and carried him a step or two before the others engulfed me. I was feeling ten foot tall and bulletproof as I took the ball for the next over, and then things got ridiculous. Jacques Rudolph was the other danger man for us and when my third ball jagged back and he got an inside edge onto the stumps … I went a little over the top.

I only bowled four overs in that spell but was cooked by the end of them. Normally I'd try to sneak another one out of the skipper but I was glad when Punter came over and suggested I might like a rest. I had nothing left – the adrenaline and emotion had spilled over and I was drained. The dressing room that night was a very 'up' place and it was no surprise that the match finished the way it did the next day with victory coming not long after lunch. Mike Hussey was a deserved man of the match for his century and great batting with the tail. For the first time, I felt that I 'got' this Test cricket caper.

The Boxing Day match was the start of a memorable month or so: Australia won the third Test in Sydney, and while I didn't repeat the Melbourne excitement, I still got to play three Tests in a row before we moved onto the VB Series against South Africa and Sri Lanka, with the first ever local Twenty20 game kicking off the limited overs part of the season.

Playing Twenty20 after a Test is a bit like slipping on the double-pluggers after wearing work boots all day – there's a certain feeling of freedom. Having said that, I'm 50-50 on Twenty20, having played it in England and now in Australia. I wasn't a fan initially – the shorter the game, the narrower the gap between good and bad teams – but you can't deny the excitement value of it, even if it's weighted more in favour of the fans than the players. I suppose it appeals to a different type of spectator – mums and dads, and kids after school – and that's got to be a good thing.

The summer ended on a high in the second ODI Final at the SCG. Australia had been beaten by Sri Lanka in the opening game of the best of three series in Adelaide, and we'd copped a bit of stick for our performance. Everyone was determined to turn it around in game two, which was do-or-die. We rose to the occasion, with the runs flowing like the Burdekin River in the wet season. That game was probably the best feeling I've had since the World Cup in 2003. I got 151 and lifted us to a score of 5-368. Like in Johannesburg, I wanted to bat right to the last over and set myself to be there at the end. We had to comprehensively win that game – 300 in my eyes wasn't enough, we had to get 310, 320 or 330 – but in the end I was that exhausted I just couldn't hit the ball over the fence again. I did a lot of running from 100 to 150, for not only myself but for Pup too, and by the end of it I was utterly stuffed. The radiator was whistling like a billy and it was ready to blow.

When I finally got out, I started to walk back in and the most extraordinary sensation swept over me as I realised the crowd were up on their feet, clapping and cheering. All the bristles stood up on the back of my neck and I thought, 'This is just amazing.' It was both humbling and exciting and easily the best feeling I'd experienced for a long, long time. I neared the edge of the field to walk up the race

When I finally got out, I started to walk back in and the most extraordinary sensation swept over me as I realised the crowd were up on their feet, clapping and cheering.

where the players go through the crowd back to the dressing rooms, when I realised how shattered I was. Everyone was still clapping but all I wanted to do was get inside and lie down before I fell down. There were a couple of security guards who escorted me up the race and they were probably just as excited as the fans. I got part of the way along and saw this bloke starting to move towards me with his arms outstretched like he was going to grab me in a bear hug. The only thing I thought was that if he got hold of me, I was going to go down, so I stuck my bat into the middle of his chest to keep him away. I admit I did it pretty emphatically – and I know now that he certainly meant no harm – but it was the only way I thought to keep him off.

It was a sensational game of cricket and was capped off by an Australian victory to level the series 1-1. But it turned out my protective instincts on the way to the dressing room created a storm that temporarily overshadowed the win. I was asked about it a few times and answered as best I could, but I couldn't help thinking to myself, 'Sorry, didn't we just put on a pretty decent score?' I've had a strange relationship with the media over the years, and don't really get their motivations sometimes. They probably say the same about me. Anyway, I reckon the people who came to the game and watched it on TV will hold dear their memories of the match, just as I will.

I never caught up with the fella I pushed, but heard that he had contacted a few media outlets to explain that he was only trying to congratulate me. If he's reading this: sorry, mate, for the misunderstanding, it was nothing personal. Hope you keep enjoying your cricket.

My innings seemed to capture the public's imagination – for mostly the right reasons – but I reckon my hair may have had something to do with it as well. The boys say the dreadlocks cover up a bald spot, but in truth, they've been a work in progress since 2004 when I got married. Actually calling them a work in progress is overstating things. I just let them grow; it's painless, though I have gone up four hat sizes with my latest Akubra. Fortunately the baggy green and my baggy Bulls cap still fit okay but the training caps are getting a bit of a strain. My hair grows naturally curly – I don't do anything special other than wash and dry it. After having quite the 'fro when I was growing up, I used to keep my hair short, although never too short because Mum would say it made me look as if I'd just got out of jail.

I'm sure some of the West Indian players enjoy having a giggle at my expense. Chris Gayle, who obviously goes to the same hairdresser as me, once asked if I was the only meat-eating Rasta in the world. But the best line came from Michael Kasprowicz. In his weekly newspaper column, Kasper suggested that following the success of the talking David Boon doll, VB should come up with a talking Roy doll for the next season. 'And what's more, when it runs out of batteries and stops talking, you can simply turn it upside down and use it to clean your toilet.'

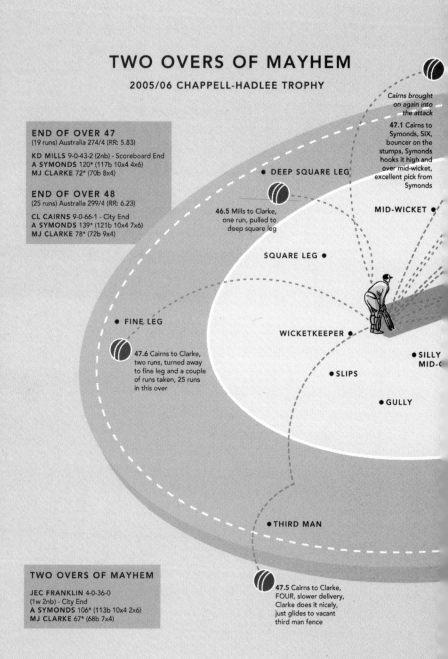

TWO OVERS OF MAYHEM

2005/06 CHAPPELL-HADLEE TROPHY

END OF OVER 47
(19 runs) Australia 274/4 (RR: 5.83)

KD MILLS 9-0-43-2 (2nb) - Scoreboard End
A SYMONDS 120* (117b 10x4 4x6)
MJ CLARKE 72* (70b 8x4)

END OF OVER 48
(25 runs) Australia 299/4 (RR: 6.23)

CL CAIRNS 9-0-66-1 - City End
A SYMONDS 139* (121b 10x4 7x6)
MJ CLARKE 78* (72b 9x4)

TWO OVERS OF MAYHEM

JEC FRANKLIN 4-0-36-0
(1w 2nb) - City End
A SYMONDS 106* (113b 10x4 2x6)
MJ CLARKE 67* (68b 7x4)

Cairns brought
on again into
the attack

47.1 Cairns to
Symonds, SIX,
bouncer on the
stumps, Symonds
hooks it high and
over mid-wicket,
excellent pick from
Symonds

DEEP SQUARE LEG

MID-WICKET

46.5 Mills to Clarke,
one run, pulled to
deep square leg

SQUARE LEG

WICKETKEEPER

FINE LEG

**SILLY
MID-O**

47.6 Cairns to Clarke,
two runs, turned away
to fine leg and a couple
of runs taken, 25 runs
in this over

SLIPS

GULLY

THIRD MAN

47.5 Cairns to Clarke,
FOUR, slower delivery,
Clarke does it nicely,
just glides to vacant
third man fence

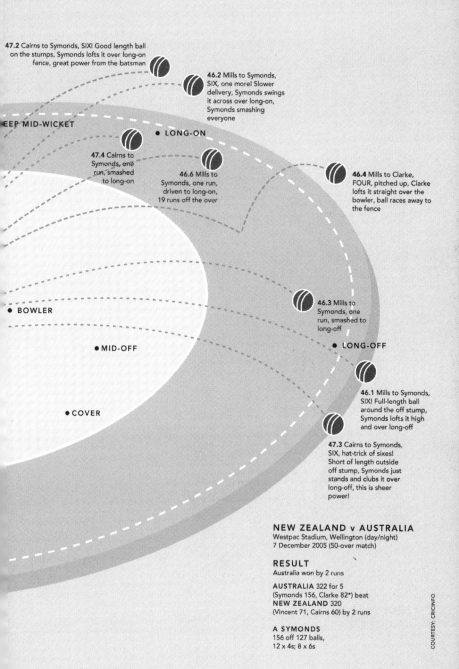

47.2 Cairns to Symonds, SIX! Good length ball on the stumps, Symonds lofts it over long-on fence, great power from the batsman

46.2 Mills to Symonds, SIX, one more! Slower delivery, Symonds swings it across over long-on, Symonds smashing everyone

EEP MID-WICKET

● LONG-ON

47.4 Cairns to Symonds, one run, smashed to long-on

46.6 Mills to Symonds, one run, driven to long-on, 19 runs off the over

46.4 Mills to Clarke, FOUR, pitched up, Clarke lofts it straight over the bowler, ball races away to the fence

46.3 Mills to Symonds, one run, smashed to long-off

● BOWLER

● MID-OFF

● LONG-OFF

46.1 Mills to Symonds, SIX! Full-length ball around the off stump, Symonds lofts it high and over long-off

● COVER

47.3 Cairns to Symonds, SIX, hat-trick of sixes! Short of length outside off stump, Symonds just stands and clubs it over long-off, this is sheer power!

NEW ZEALAND v AUSTRALIA
Westpac Stadium, Wellington (day/night)
7 December 2005 (50-over match)

RESULT
Australia won by 2 runs

AUSTRALIA 322 for 5
(Symonds 156, Clarke 82*) beat
NEW ZEALAND 320
(Vincent 71, Cairns 60) by 2 runs

A SYMONDS
156 off 127 balls,
12 x 4s; 8 x 6s

COURTESY: CRICINFO

CHAPTER 16

BLOOD IN THE WATER

Seeing your own blood pooling on the ground in front of you is one of the most alarming experiences imaginable. On this particular occasion, I'd just been hit in the face by a cricket ball travelling at more than 100 km/h, but the funny thing was, there was no real pain. At least at the time. We were playing the Proteas in the second Test in Durban in South Africa in April 2006, it was late on the opening day, and the crowd had been baying for my blood. When Makhaya Ntini got a short one to jag back towards me, I guess they got what they wanted.

Over the years I'd copped the odd ball on the scone – it's an occupational hazard we all have to deal with – but I didn't wear a helmet until my second season with Queensland in 1995/96, preferring to bat in a floppy hat (a la Richie Richardson) or nothing at all. I'd been lucky, but I put a lot of it down to the rigorous coaching Dad gave me as a kid, even though I probably didn't appreciate it at the time. He used to terrorise me on occasion and I'd wake up thinking, 'Oh no, he's going to do the short pitch stuff again this morning. He'll hit me in the head for sure!' But he really was a great teacher, and would break things down, ensuring you mastered them one at a time before moving on to the next. When it came to short-pitched balls – bumpers and bouncers – we spent a long time on the dos and don'ts. Thankfully, I learned pretty quickly, although when he'd say we were going to work on pulls and cut shots, I prayed I wouldn't mix them up.

The one that got me in Durban was a pretty fair nut. I'd scored a couple of runs but was intent on surviving the last few overs in what were less than ideal batting conditions. The light was bad – it was gloomy even though the floodlights were on – the ball was hard to see, and as Ntini's action can angle it back at you from time to time, you've got to be vigilant. He'd hit Justin Langer during the first Test with an unreadable ball and the one that got me certainly seamed off the track. On the replay you can see that I dropped my hands to let it go, but it came back at me and caught me right between my lips and my nose, pushing my helmet grill back into my face. I've no real beef with Ntini as it was partly my fault: my grill had been getting gradually closer and closer to my face due to the length and bulk of my hair and Pup had even noticed and told me I should adjust it. Of course I didn't. More's the pity.

It turned out my teeth had gone through my lip, my nose was bleeding, my front teeth were loose and a bottom tooth was chipped. I thought for a second he'd knocked some of them out: I couldn't feel them which was why I was a bit panicky. I couldn't help thinking, 'Oh no, how I am going to look now, with my two front teeth gone?'

Our physio, Alex Kountouri, came out onto the pitch to try and tidy me up and stop the bleeding, and Mike Hussey – who was batting with me – gently suggested that maybe I should go off. 'There aren't any heroes out here, mate,' he said. 'Head off and get fixed up and come back tomorrow.'

But I wasn't going anywhere. I'd come to the wicket after Brett Lee had got out and as I walked onto the field Andre Nel had given me a massive spray about being scared. I may have been bloody-minded, but there was no way I was taking a backward step. I was also thinking of the bloke coming in after me: you don't want one of your mates seeing your blood on the pitch. I told Huss and Alex that I'd be right in a minute; I was toey, but Alex made sure I took my time. Ntini didn't bowl a short one the next ball but he did give me one more in that spell. I survived through to stumps that night, although my biggest test came after play. I swelled up like a beetroot and ended up with three stitches inside my lip and two on the outside – stiff, sore and ridiculous to look at. Of course, once the boys were sure I was okay, it was pretty well open season.

<hr/>

During a practice session in the West Indies a few years earlier, I'd belted a delivery from Brad Hogg up into the top of the nets which hit a cable and deflected straight into his face. He went down like he'd been shot. I didn't know what I'd done – bashed his teeth in, broken his nose, smashed his jaw? I ran up in a panic and turned him over but he was okay – his nose was straight, his teeth were all still there, and he was conscious. It could have been a lot worse: it had got him exactly the same place as me – just below his nose – and before you could say, 'bigger than a balloon' his top lip had swollen to three or four times its normal size. If you've ever seen the remake of the *Nutty Professor* starring Eddie Murphy, then you'll appreciate why the boys nicknamed him Sherman Klumpp. Because everything was so tight and swollen, we just had to try to make him laugh. Poor bugger – he couldn't eat properly, talk properly or smile …

So here I was in exactly the same position, and having dished it out, of course I had to cop it. I was sure I was going to pop my stitches and had to put my hand over my top lip and hold it together when the boys got me laughing. When I ran I could feel my lip bouncing up and down and it was five days before I could eat solids.

Sherman Klumpp jokes aside, the next morning when I went back out onto the pitch, it was on again: Ntini was coming in hard and the South Africans were putting plenty of pressure on us. I stuck around for about 90 minutes, and while we didn't score a heap of runs, it was vital we occupied the crease and didn't collapse. I eventually got out just before lunch, but Huss continued to bat beautifully, going on to partner Warney, Kasper and Stuey Clark and lifting us into a solid position. Buck told me later that he thought it was my best Test innings, even if the scorebook shows I only contributed 13.

It was a tough old match both on and off the field; neither side gave an inch and the tension that had been brewing since South Africa toured Australia over Christmas and the New Year threatened to bubble over. Their captain Graeme Smith had stirred things up during the summer but his form slump meant that he'd left himself wide open. There had been a fair bit of crowd unrest and a few complaints from the Proteas about racial vilification. Going to South Africa, I did wonder how we'd fare on the boundary if the locals got worked up, but you can't let it get to you and you certainly can't go whinging to the skipper every time someone calls you a name. I've

For whatever reason, the South Africans took a dislike to me, and although I found them a bit humourless on occasion, I could understand why they sometimes react the way they do.

had my share of slurs over the years but nothing that's got me all that riled up. I'm not at all sensitive about the whole skin colour issue, but I know it's different for others, and racism doesn't belong in cricket, or anywhere else for that matter.

For whatever reason, the South Africans took a dislike to me, and although I found them a bit humourless on occasion, I could understand why they sometimes react the way they do. They cop a lot at home – their ex-players can be pretty harsh and so can their media – and even to an outsider there appeared to be a degree of turmoil within their ranks.

Given all this, it's hardly surprising that when a whiff of scandal hit the papers concerning my 'alleged nightclub scuffle' with Graeme Smith, just about everyone thought I was guilty as charged. To set the record straight, Graeme and I did not even exchange a sharp glance, let alone a harsh word, on the night in question. But it is true I found myself in the midst of an unnecessary drama at the club where the trouble was alleged to have taken place. A few of us were in the VIP section celebrating our win after the first Test, and we happened to bump into a few members of the Cheetahs Super 12 rugby union team. I was happily chatting away to Springbok prop Ollie Le Roux – as big a unit as I've ever met – when another Cheetahs player a little further down the bar decided he wasn't that struck on me. There were a few hard stares exchanged, a bit like two bulls marking out their turf, until at some point I decided enough was enough and asked this fella whether he wanted to take it outside. I was on my way out of the VIP area when Pup zoomed in to steer me away and calm things down. Big Ollie did his bit to keep everyone happy too and after the red mist had faded and I was in a more receptive frame of mind, Pup convinced me that I'd be better off leaving and finishing the celebrations elsewhere.

I owe Pup big time. Looking back, I realise now I was headed for the sort of strife that could have brought a swift end to my tour and possibly my international career. It was a sobering reminder that the old-school ways where two men sort out their differences one-on-one are long gone. It's unacceptable for high-profile athletes to be punching on, whether inside a club or out – we're ambassadors for our country and have a responsibility to respect the cap and uphold the spirit of the game, not to mention provide good role models for aspiring kids. While it can be all too easy to forget this in the heat of the moment – and regrettably few of us have spotless records – there's no excuse for being a boofhead.

The Proteas had gone into the First Test in Cape Town on a high after their victory in the fifth and final One Day International in Johannesburg. I'd missed the start of the tour with a hip injury which meant I was on the sideline for the Twenty20 game and three of the five ODIs, but I got it sorted and scored 76 from roughly the same number of balls in the fourth ODI in Durban. Returning to Wanderers Stadium for the fifth match was a buzz, even if the shoe was soon to be on the other foot.

It all began beautifully with Ricky Ponting leading the way with a sensational 164. Everyone else then followed the leader: Gilly hit 55 from 44 balls; Simon Katich cruised to 79 from 90; Huss cleared the pickets three times on the way to 81 off 51 and I added 27 from 13 as we posted a then world record ODI score of 434. I'm not talking out of school when I say that we were pretty confident we were home and hosed once the innings finished and it's no surprise that we carried on a like a mob of gooses.

Pumped and confident, we came out after the break thinking we'd get a few quick ones and be on the fizz early, and when Boeta Dippenaar went for one in the second over, you could almost taste the Castle Lagers. But Graeme Smith, who'd had a tough old time of it, turned a corner and started belting balls like he was trying to win the game single-handedly. What was good for the skipper was good for Herschelle Gibbs who followed suit, teeing off from almost the first ball and piercing the field every time. Even when he shanked it, he found a gap! At first we told ourselves it was just a fluke, we'd get on them soon, but after it happened again and again, you could see the brows starting to furrow. We needed a wicket, the run rate wasn't going up, but we didn't know what to try. More pace or less pace on the ball; more aggressive fields or more defensive fields?

Smith fell in the 23rd for 90 off just 55 balls, but by then the Proteas were 2-190. Herschelle just kept powering on and even though we nabbed a few scalps, every batsman was scoring at better than a run a ball. As it got shorter and shorter, you could see them starting to think they could win it.

We could well and truly forget about those beers!

We finally got Gibbs, but only after he had scored an heroic 175 off just 111 balls, before Mark Boucher and Makhaya Ntini dug in

and passed our total on the last ball of the innings. It was a shocking way to end a game as far as we were concerned, but it was undeniably good cricket for the punters, no two ways about it.

After the excitement and disappointment of South Africa, the prospect of heading to Bangladesh for Test and One Day Internationals didn't have many of us doing high fives, but I had a point to prove, and although a lengthy off-season was attractive, I was keener still to see if I could further better my Test standing. Part of me also wanted to make up for the last time Bangladesh and Australia had gone into battle. This time I vowed I'd tackle them with a clearer head.

ROY'S HIGHEST SCORES
LIST A/ONE DAY

07/12/2005
ODI, AUSTRALIA v NEW ZEALAND, WELLINGTON

RUNS	BALLS	6's	STK-RT
156	127	8	122.38

12/02/2006
ODI, AUSTRALIA v SRI LANKA, SYDNEY

RUNS	BALLS	6's	STK-RT
151	127	3	118.90

06/06/2004
LEAGUE, KENT v LANCASHIRE, TUNBRIDGE WELLS

RUNS	BALLS	6's	STK-RT
146	110	4	132.72

11/02/2003
ODI, AUSTRALIA v PAKISTAN, JOHANNESBURG

RUNS	BALLS	6's	STK-RT
143*	125	2	114.40

22/08/2005
LEAGUE, LANCASHIRE v GLOUCESTERSHIRE, MANCHESTER

RUNS	BALLS	6's	STK-RT
129	107	2	120.56

04/09/2004
ODI, AUSTRALIA v PAKISTAN, LORD'S

RUNS	BALLS	6's	STK-RT
104*	103	1	100.97

COURTESY: ROSS DUNDAS

ROY'S HIGHEST SCORES LIST A

26/04/2006
ODI, AUSTRALIA v BANGLADESH, FATULLAH

RUNS	BALLS	6's	STK-RT
103*	125	2	82.40

15/07/2005
C&G, LANCASHIRE v SUSSEX, MANCHESTER

RUNS	BALLS	6's	STK-RT
101	121	1	83.47

03/05/1999
CGU, KENT v LEICESTERSHIRE, CANTERBURY

RUNS	BALLS	6's	STK-RT
95			

11/08/2003
LEAGUE, KENT v WORCESTERSHIRE, CANTERBURY

RUNS	BALLS	6's	STK-RT
93	82	4	113.41

21/10/2001
ING,QUEENSLAND v WESTERN AUSTRALIA, BRISBANE

RUNS	BALLS	6's	STK-RT
91	57	2	159.65

18/03/2003
ODI, AUSTRALIA v SRI LANKA, PORT ELIZABETH

RUNS	BALLS	6's	STK-RT
91*	118	1	77.12

A ROSE BY ANY OTHER NAME

By Michael Kasprowicz

On a tour to South Africa a few years back, we visited a vineyard near Cape Town. At the end of each row of vines was a rose bush; they plant them as a type of early warning system as roses are susceptible to many of the same type of fungal diseases as grape vines but show their signs earlier, allowing the grower to treat the vines before the disease takes hold.

Not knowing this, Roy looked at the spectacular sight of so many rose bushes and rows of vines and asked a strangely logical question: 'So is that where *Rosé* comes from?'

BEST ONE DAY INTERNATIONAL STRIKE-RATES

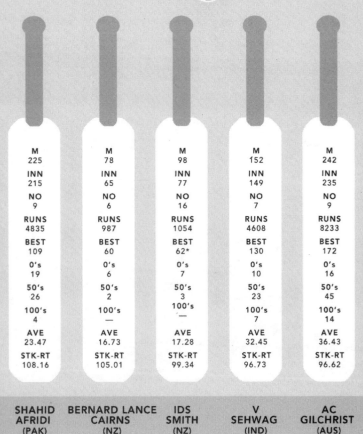

	SHAHID AFRIDI (PAK)	BERNARD LANCE CAIRNS (NZ)	IDS SMITH (NZ)	V SEHWAG (IND)	AC GILCHRIST (AUS)
M	225	78	98	152	242
INN	215	65	77	149	235
NO	9	6	16	7	9
RUNS	4835	987	1054	4608	8233
BEST	109	60	62*	130	172
0's	19	6	7	10	16
50's	26	2	3	23	45
100's	4	—	—	7	14
AVE	23.47	16.73	17.28	32.45	36.43
STK-RT	108.16	105.01	99.34	96.73	96.62

BEST ONE DAY INTERNATIONAL STRIKE-RATES

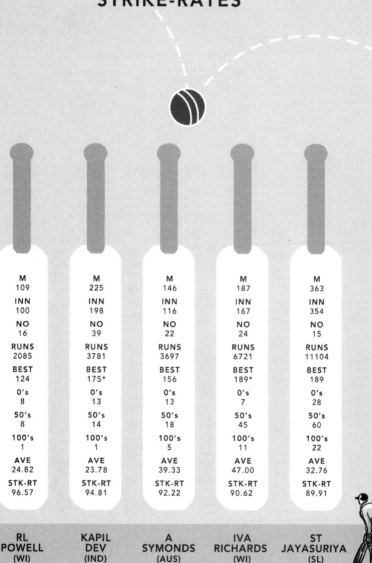

	RL POWELL (WI)	KAPIL DEV (IND)	A SYMONDS (AUS)	IVA RICHARDS (WI)	ST JAYASURIYA (SL)
M	109	225	146	187	363
INN	100	198	116	167	354
NO	16	39	22	24	15
RUNS	2085	3781	3697	6721	11104
BEST	124	175*	156	189*	189
0's	8	13	13	7	28
50's	8	14	18	45	60
100's	1	1	5	11	22
AVE	24.82	23.78	39.33	47.00	32.76
STK-RT	96.57	94.81	92.22	90.62	89.91

CHAPTER 17

GET YOUR
MOTOR RUNNING

As I suspected, the trip to Bangladesh in April 2006 straight after the South African series was a tour too far for some. Funnily enough, I wasn't that bothered, mainly because there were Test matches to play and because I'd gotten used to the subcontinent after my first few rocky visits. You've got to go with the flow I reckon, especially in India, Pakistan, Bangladesh and Sri Lanka where there are literally millions of cricketing fans who all want a piece of you. Sometimes it seems like your every waking moment is of interest to someone. In India, you'd get up in the morning, throw open the curtains of your hotel to check out the weather, and look down to see a mob of people waving and cheering like you'd just scored a century. It reminds me of that scene in Monty Python's *Life of Brian* when the 'Messiah' walks out of the cave to see thousands of people gathered just to catch a glimpse of him. Some players have a hard time dealing with this sort of 'rock star' level of interest and keep to their rooms when they're not on the field. Fair enough, but I try and make the best of it and treat it as an opportunity because who knows when I'll be back.

On one trip to India we were invited to visit a real-life Maharajah at his palace. The invitation had said 'casual dress' and so I followed that to a tee – I wore a singlet, footy shorts and thongs, which I'm sure wasn't exactly the look they were expecting. In any event, we were welcomed warmly and treated like, well kings. The Maharajah wasn't that old and loved his cricket but I was just as impressed with his digs: there was a long table that had a model train running around it carrying the various crystal decanters of drinks. I could see myself with one of those, as long as I could work out how to keep them cold …

I really like the Bangladeshis too. A lot of them have had tough upbringings and it can't have been easy getting to where they are now. Even though I still want to be on the winning side whenever we play them, I can't help admiring their guts and determination. Their cheeky little batsman Mohammad Ashraful is a terrific bloke and when we first came up against him Pup and I gave him heaps. He was just a teenager back then, but I can tell you he gave as good as he got and totally won us over. The other bloke I have a soft spot for is Mohammad Rafique, their fiercely determined left-arm spinner who in my estimation has got to be one of their best players. He comes from a very poor background but does a lot to look after his extended family: he owns a clothing factory that employs a fair few people and has turned his cricketing talent into something that benefits his countrymen and -women. We usually talk fishing when our paths cross and he's invited me to stay the next time I'm in Bangladesh, which hopefully I'll get a chance to do one of these days.

Bangladesh gave Australia a good run for our money in the 2006 Test matches. I didn't get a look in for the first two, and so had to watch from the sidelines as the Bangers almost pinched an upset in the first before Punter shepherded us to a three-wicket win. Then Jason 'Dizzy' Gillespie took the accepted wisdom of the cricket world (that nightwatchmen are yesterday's men) turned it on its head and scored an incredible 201 not out in the second. I still can't quite believe that one – more power to him though and just as with Glenn McGrath a few seasons before, getting an uncharacteristically good Test score means the dressing-room dynamics swing back in favour of the bowlers when it comes to bragging rights with the bat.

The one-dayers ended in a 3-0 win to Australia, and I can't tell you how relieved I was to score a century in the second game to get us a series win. Our tour was a bit of a 'crystal ball experience' for Australian cricket with the likes of Mark Cosgrove, Dan Cullen, James Hopes, Mitchell Johnson and Brett Dorey playing and playing well. But I couldn't help looking back, specifically to Cardiff, and while a working-class hundred in Fatullah 12 months later couldn't make up for my indiscretions, it at least set things partially right. As far as hundreds go, that one was my slowest but most responsible. We were in a bit of strife at 3-10 when I went in, and I survived a big shout first ball, but with the support of Pup, we were able to put the innings back on track. It wasn't easy – it was a dead pitch and their slow bowlers, especially Rafique, really tied us down.

I half-suspect Pup wanted me to stay in the middle a bit longer so we could discuss our holiday plans for when we got back home. He's from the western suburbs of Sydney and is a young bloke with plenty of confidence: there's the diamond in the ear, a bit of bling here and there and some good blond tips up top. He's a cheeky bugger too; he never forgets to remind me that the first time I saw him on a field, I sledged him. He was playing for NSW so as far as I was concerned, he was fair game. I was out towards the boundary but I made sure he heard me. Although on the surface you might think we're like chalk and cheese, we've become great mates in recent times and have a fair bit in common: we're both very close to our families and grew up learning about the game in a similar way; and we both play aggressive, attacking cricket.

When you're on a long tour with time on your hands you find yourself cooking up all sorts of wild plans for when you get home, most of which of course go absolutely nowhere. Usually when a tour ends, those of us who aren't playing in England peel off to our respective homes or hideaways and get on with 'regular' life for a while. I don't remember where it began, but by the end of our Bangladeshi tour Pup and I had planned an off-season, big-time adventure road trip for when we got home. It was one of those conversations that started with, 'Imagine if we could ...' and ended with us working out that we could hire a campervan in Sydney, drive it up to Brisbane, and then fly to Ingham for a spot of real-man hunting and fishing. Neither of us was going to England in the off-season and with no playing commitments until at least September, it seemed like the perfect mid-year plan. Now it might seem strange that after spending several weeks living in each other's pockets we'd be planning to spend another week sharing a campervan as soon as we got back, but opportunities like this just don't come up every day ...

Pup was fine with the driving-to-Brisbane part of the deal, but was apprehensive about the hunting and fishing. He was a bit of a bush virgin and having heard plenty of daring dressing-room tales of fierce boars and lurking monster crocs, I could understand his concern. Nevertheless, he was keen to experience it all, and I knew that my mates Anthony 'Yogi' Fortini and Mick Sheehan would look after him well.

Before the fun started, I had a couple of serious things to sort out. During our contract chats with Cricket Australia not long after we got back, I was told politely but firmly that I had one last chance in terms of my behaviour. CEO James Sutherland was quite clear that this latest contract would be ripped up if I overstepped the mark again. I asked them what would happen if one of the boys got into strife and I weighed in to 'help' them out. To his credit, James heard me out, but his reply was blunt – I had to learn to protect myself and by that, he wasn't talking physically. 'Don't put yourself in a spot where you can get in trouble. If it develops – walk away.' I've given this wise advice a lot of thought and intend to put it into practice; if I don't, I won't be playing for Australia again.

◀▮▶

After that was sorted, it was back to the road trip. Pup and I argued over who'd get the bunk and who'd get the main bed, but once the door of our Winnebago was slammed shut, I left all my worries behind and we headed out onto the wide-open road. Despite our lengthy 'planning' sessions, we did overlook a few essentials. For starters, our map was of all Australia, so we had the big picture, but little else. It also meant we had to follow our noses and look for helpful road signs whenever we got to one of the places we wanted to visit. I lost count of the number of U-turns we did when we wandered into a town that neither of us had been to, so you could say we moved at a 'leisurely' pace. We stopped at Newcastle, Port Macquarie, Coffs Harbour and Byron Bay, as well as a few nice spots in between, to have a dip, wet a line or wet the whistle. Or sometimes all three. We caught up with Pup's Auntie and his Nan and Pop in Coffs and had a bit of a fish and a night out at the RSL with them. We even scored a prize spot at Byron Bay at the First Sun Caravan park – right at the front overlooking the beach – and so we really did catch the first rays that morning. This part of the trip lasted about five days and was a beaut way to wind down.

We took to the air next, flying to Ingham to stay with Yogi and his wife Jo and kids Melise and Aiden. Yogi was a groomsman at my wedding and I'm godfather to the two little ones and it's a responsibility I try to take as seriously as I can. Yogi runs his own cane harvesting business and whenever I go there I see it at its best.

Me and a Herbert River Barra!

Everyone works extra hard before I arrive to get their jobs done and clear a bit of 'play' time. I've always fancied the idea of owning a property and back when I was tossing up giving rugby league a go, I sought Yogi's advice as to whether I should move up north and settle there. He told me not to be stupid and pointed out that I was doing something that thousands of people would give their right arms to do. I could muck around with cattle and cane anytime I liked once I finished with cricket, but I shouldn't even contemplate giving it up now. Thanks, Yogi, good advice!

My other mate up north, Mick Sheehan, runs the 400,000 hectare Esmeralda Station, which is south of Croydon in the Gulf of Carpentaria. Esmeralda's got to be one of the best places on the planet: there's fishing, pig hunting, bull catching … it's an adventure from sun-up to sundown, and then it's an adventure until the sun comes up again! Bull catching is a buzz, even though I'm sure its bloody hard work for the blokes who have to do it for a living. These days they use helicopters to flush them out of the scrub onto the flats and then use two bull-catcher vehicles and quad bikes – it's on like Donkey Kong tying to get them sometimes.

Mick had picked up a new helicopter not long before Pup and I arrived and we'd barely settled in at Yogi's when we heard the sound of the blades. It takes about two hours to fly to Mick's, compared to about six or seven hours' driving, but the trip is well worth it if you've got the time. We went for a bit of a fish in the Gulf while we were there but unfortunately the cyclones and the wet weather put a dampener on most of the pig chasing and the like because it was simply too boggy to get after them, even with quad bikes and four-wheel drives. Notwithstanding the rain it was a sensational trip. We even managed to give the locals at the Croydon Hotel something to talk about when we popped in for a few light refreshments on the way back to Esmeralda one afternoon. If you've got one, you can land your chopper across the road from the pub, which is one of those old-style outback hotels, and I can highly recommend the hospitality.

▄▄▌▌▐▄

With Roy and Pup's 'Big Adventure' over, and my trusty travelling companion heading home to the relative safety of Sydney, there were just a few outstanding matters for me to take care of before 2006/07 pre-season training kicked off. This book was the first priority. The second was getting my wrist seen to and so on the advice of Cricket Australia doctor Trefor James I arranged to have some exploratory surgery performed in Melbourne. I can't recall exactly where or when I'd injured it, but there was some floating bone which needed seeing to. The surgeon, Greg Hoy, did a good job although it was probably more extensive than I thought it was going to be. Luckily, I've always been a quick healer and despite chafing at the bit while I waited for the green light to start rehabilitation (and get back to lifting crab pots out of the water again), it came good pretty swiftly. Sorting it out meant I could get into the nets again to work on a few remedial things with my batting that I had wanted to deal with for a while. It was like turning the clock back to the old days, hitting heaps of balls on the bowling machine, and it was a reminder of where my cricketing career had begun.

What really brought home just how far I'd come was being invited to front Queensland Cricket's junior sign-on campaign. A poster showing Aussie cricketer Jodie Purves and me demonstrating various cricketing moves was produced and I was asked to come up

Where it all began – the nets at All Souls at Charters Towers.

with some one-line hints. As I jotted them down, I felt like a seven-year-old again, back in the All Souls nets in Charters Towers, with Dad banging the ball into the well-worn concrete, reminding me to watch it, step to it and swing positively. I hope there'll be kids out there who will stick that poster on their wall and have the same sort of fun with their family learning to play as I was lucky enough to have with mine. Because let's face it, I'm where I am today because my family went the extra mile – they fostered my love of the game, sacrificed a lot to give me the chances I needed and supported me through the good and the bad. And if my noggin on a poster can help someone else get to where I am, then I reckon I'll be pretty happy with what I've achieved.

CHAPTER 18

THE 2006/07 ASHES SERIES

'Uh oh, I'm in trouble again.' That was the first thought that flashed through my head when I got an unexpected call from Cricket Australia on 10 December 2006. It was my day off and I'd been fishing at Jacobs Well, a beautiful little spot at the southern end of Moreton Bay. I'd checked the crab pots and was hauling my boat out of the water when the mobile went berserk.

It was Michael Brown, general manager of Cricket Ops.

And he said he had *good* news.

Hmm. Someone must have contacted him with a sponsorship proposal. Better than a poke in the eye with a burnt stick. At least I wasn't in the gun again.

But then Brownie delivered the punch line, and it was one out of the box.

Jumping for joy (and being caught by Haydos)
upon reaching my first Test ton in Melbourne on
27 December 2006. A moment I'll never ever forget.

'Roy, you've been picked for the Perth Test.'

I almost fell over: flabbergasted and gobsmacked don't even come close. I muddled through the rest of the confab but I was in total shock. I was also on my own. With no one around to share my good news, I quickly pulled it all together, jumped in the ute and tore off home through the cane fields, uttering a fair few 'yahoos' (plus a bit extra) along the way.

Life's funny like that: one minute you're going about your business and the next – BAM! – you're flipped upside down. In the weeks prior to getting the call from Brownie, I had started to wonder whether I'd get the chance to wear my baggy green during what was shaping up to be an historic Ashes Series. I'll admit it, on occasion I may have even got a bit emotional. Tidying up the house one day, I'd dug out my cap and had a good old sniff. It smelled of beer, sweat and great times. I must have told someone, because soon enough the press found out about it and had a field day. It *was* a bit of a laugh, especially as the ICC had just launched 'The Fragrance of the ICC World Cup 2007', the game's first official perfume! I bet it didn't smell nearly as good as my baggy green.

I'd been enjoying playing for the Bulls with my old mates Mahbo, Hopesy and Bic. One day, we got to chatting to Michael Buchanan (son of the Australian coach, John) in the dressing room, and while we suspected he might have a tip on who'd make the cut for the third Test, we were focused on getting the Bulls closer to another Pura Cup win. I may have casually asked Michael to give his old man a call for a heads-up – I honestly can't remember – but he's a cool customer and to his credit gave absolutely nothing away. A definite chip off the old block.

With the benefit of hindsight, given the two 'hiccups' between the second and third Tests, I must have had a sneaking suspicion I was in the frame. Damien Martyn's shock retirement straight after Adelaide had left us all on the back foot – he'd made a huge contribution to the game over the years and would be greatly missed, but he'd clearly made up his mind and there was no going back.

Shane Watson, on the other hand, was just plain unlucky. He'd had back troubles in 2003 and then did his shoulder big-time playing against the Windies last season. Poor bloke couldn't take a trick. His international career seemed weirdly linked to mine and I couldn't help thinking how my ups so often coincided with his downs. I made a mental note to get in touch with him as soon as I got to Perth and give him a kick along. Watto works as hard at his game as anyone, and for as long as I've known him has been hungering after the chance to get a good run at Test and ODI level to prove himself once and for all. I knew only too well how disappointed he must have been feeling.

◼⫴▶

Making the squad was one thing, but actually getting a start was another. I knew I still had a lot of work to do: my fielding had been good, my bowling okay, but I hadn't set any records with my batting. I felt physically fit though and I was confident I had the right attitude too. In my book, there's not much more that I can do than that.

Things really started to liven up when I did a press conference in Perth on 11 December and a journo decided to pin me down with the old 'born in Birmingham, selected for England A, what *are* ya?' routine. I was probably a bit sharp with him (apparently I was 'fuming') but in all honesty it was as clear to me then as it was back in 1995 that even though I might look different, I'm as Aussie as John Williamson eating a Vegemite sandwich in a drought. And I've never felt any other way.

They also suggested that perhaps I didn't quite have the right 'temperament' for Test cricket (or for press conferences, but that's another story). There was no doubt I'd had more chances than an alley cat and more recalls than a dud car, but I reckoned this Ashes Series was different. I could feel it in my bones. Firstly, I'd played against pretty much all of the English team during my career and while I was good mates with a few of them and respected them as a squad, I certainly didn't fear them. Secondly, the Australian Test team was in menacing form, both physically and mentally: they were front-page news almost every day (for one reason or another) and were up a comfortable two-zip when I came into the side. And thirdly, after the press were through with me, the focus shifted squarely onto the shoulders of the young West Australian Adam Voges, which allowed me to step out of the spotlight and concentrate on knuckling down.

I think most of the boys were pleased to have me back in the dressing room and it wasn't long before I managed to get them laughing. Brett Lee was anxious about the impending (and late) arrival of his first child, so being a knockabout man of the world, I suggested to him that maybe the Doc could seduce the baby, you know, to speed things up. I knew I meant to say *induce* – I've been around enough expectant dads to know the lingo, fellas – but as per usual the two words got mixed up in the delivery. Lucky for me young Preston arrived on track without any special seduction needed for either him or his mum!

Jokes aside, the third Test was do-or-die for England, and the pressure was on right from the get-go. Despite the pre-match questions over the state of the famed WACA wicket, it turned out to be a very nice batting strip. In our first innings, Mike Hussey and Justin Langer loosened things up, and Pup was looking strong before Steve Harmison got him with a clever caught-and-bowled. Then it was my turn; this was it. I'd been out there for a while and was just getting into a groove when I tried to belt a long hop off Monty Panesar. It was a ball I'm sure I would have smacked for four on any other day, but I over-hit it, got a nick, and that was that. Out for an ordinary 26 off 30 balls.

I was kicking myself – I'd wasted a golden opportunity. Fortunately, I managed to pick up a couple of wickets – including that of skipper and good mate Freddy Flintoff – when we went into field. But my relief was short-lived: in our second batting dig, Monty got me *again*, this time for a miserable two runs. I'd faced him in England on turning pitches when he was playing for Northamptonshire, but this was my first real look at him on Australian soil and he was proving to be a handful. I hadn't set out to take him on, but I knew I had to refocus, play my way and put it back on England when my next chance came around.

In the end we romped it home. Huss, Pup and Gilly tore through them; Stuart Clark was on fire and Warney reached an amazing 699 wickets. What a way to end a Test. The scorecard tells one side of the story, but I can vouch that being part of the team that regained the Ashes was a priceless, humbling and utterly unforgettable experience. I enjoyed the celebrations as much as anyone, but I know it meant the world to the blokes who'd been in the cut and thrust in England in 2005.

Punter and Buck stressed to us that 3-0 up didn't mean we could let down our guards and it was expected that we'd crack on at full-strength in the final two. There was no chance of any complacency on my part – I had a point to prove to myself and a job to do for the team. Buck had been extra supportive throughout and I sensed the boys wanted me to do well too. With the amount of good luck messages I got, it felt as if the whole country was behind me.

There's been a bit of talk about 'scriptwriters' and the like, particularly regarding Warney's amazing ride, but when I look back, I would never in a million years have predicted that the 2006 Boxing Day Test was about to surpass the one just 12 months before. Fair enough, this time round the occasion was massive, the crowd enormous, the sense of anticipation almost overwhelming, but I've learned the hard way never to take things for granted.

Victoria was hit with a freak cold snap on Christmas Day and when Boxing Day dawned, I could have sworn I was back in Gloucestershire it was that bleak. It certainly didn't bother Victoria's favourite son though and in years to come when they discuss the annals of Australian cricket, I reckon 26 December 2006 will be known as 'Shane Warne Day'. Warney notched up a tidy 5-39 off just 17 and a bit overs – great figures in any arena – but the ball which gave him his 700th was truly something else and would have got *any* batsman out. Andy Strauss just happened to be the unlucky bloke facing. It was a proud moment for every Aussie cricketer, and one that I was privileged to have been a part of.

I felt much, much better on the field than I had in years, not that my new relaxed and comfortable approach helped when it was my turn to bat on day two. Australia was in a spot of bother at 5-84 and despite having the reassuring figure of Matty Hayden at the other end, it took me about three years to get off the mark. I was stiff and tentative and a bit unlucky: even when I absolutely crunched a half volley on leg stump in one of the early overs, it went straight to midwicket. I was ready for a fight though – I didn't care how I got them but I was going to get them – and I kept telling myself that if I hung in there, eventually I'd scrounge some runs from somewhere.

Steve Harmison and Freddy were bowling well and weren't giving me much room to move, but when Kevin Pietersen chimed in with a few lines about me being 'the specialist fielder' it might just have been a blessing in disguise. Haydos was like a Red Heeler with a fresh bone and as I finally got going, he didn't miss a chance to remind old KP that 'there's another one for the specialist fielder'.

Unlike the 2005 Series, where England capitalised on every opportunity and seemed to somehow sway the natural order, this time the cards were all falling our way. I had a really close call when sweeping on 50 – I was plumb LBW, actually – but I hit the ground too which made a woody sound and luckily for me, Rudi Koertzen didn't budge. When lunch rolled around, I was sitting on four, and although I didn't really want to break the concentration, it was actually quite useful. I had a bit of tucker and even managed to catch my fishing segment on the Cricket Show that Channel Nine had done with me earlier. Then I put on a new pair of socks and new batting inners straight out of the packet – it's superstitious, I know, but it genuinely helps me feel refreshed – and took a few deep breaths.

When we got going again, time just seemed to fly: it was like we were in a bubble. Haydos doesn't look at the scoreboard all that much while he's batting, so when he reached his ton, it was a surprise for us all. I was light on with my congratulations and felt a bit rude, but Haydos didn't care and wasn't that worked up himself –

he was more worried about me. He told me when he reached his 150 that he purposely toned down the celebrations for his ton so that I wouldn't get too distracted.

We made it to tea with him on a century and me getting up around 70. In a sense, the session had been like prepping for a huge party. We'd got the place tidied up, the beers cold, the barbie hot and now it was time to kick back and enjoy ourselves.

***

Harmison and Freddy came back pretty hard early in the next session and we had a tough period early on, but then suddenly the English boys became wobbly and undecided – they set the fields defensively and there were some easy runs on offer. We were knocking Monty around a bit – ones and twos mostly – and when I noticed Paul Collingwood warming up, it was clear they were in dire straits and were scratching around for other options. It was also clear that if we kept a steady hand, we'd have them.

I got into the 90s without too much drama and then took a four off Monty to go to 96. Collingwood was up next and I decided the smart thing to do would be to just knock the runs off in tidy little singles. Haydos picked up one and I was on strike again. In spite of my sensible intentions, a little voice inside my head just wouldn't shut up …

'If he throws one up in the zone, go him and give it some Larry Dooley straight back over his head!'

I wasn't going to fight myself and decided that if he *did* slip one up there I'd play a good strong shot and just see what happened. Of course, sometimes you decide on a plan but before you know it, you're walking back to the rooms feeling dirty on everyone and everything.

Luckily this time that wasn't the case. Collingwood lobbed it up, I gave it a bit of SW and as soon as it connected, I knew it had cleared the fielder. I didn't know it was six – I just knew I was there.

And then I lost it: relief, joy and excitement tumbled over me and I was overcome with a hundred mixed thoughts and emotions. My grandfather, who'd died earlier in the year, had been at the 'G the previous Boxing Day, and so I yelled up to the sky, 'That's for you, Grandad!'. It was special all right. Up the other end was my big mate Haydos. He'd been an absolute rock throughout the entire innings, not to mention much of my professional career, and I was just so pumped I leapt into his arms, inadvertently squashing his helmet back into his face and giving him a late Christmas pressie of a nice little blood blister. Sorry, mate!

A split second later the real world rushed back in. It's like when you've been underwater and resurface quickly and your senses explode: there's this roar in your ears and everything goes in and out of focus; it's an almost indescribable sensation but it's one that I'll never forget.

I had all my family there that day – Mum, Dad, Nick and Louise, my uncle and auntie, plus a heap of friends – so I knew the moment was being shared by the people I loved. That said, Dad had stayed true to form, spending most of the day in the MCG car park, determined not to jinx me. He did catch a bit of it, but only when he was satisfied that I'd played myself in. Luckily he was watching when I reached 100. I know he was rapt that all of those balls he'd thrown me over the years had finally resulted in a Test ton. I had 118 messages on my mobile that night – from mates and people from all over the place. I didn't get to reply to many of them but I read every one – and some a few times over.

Believe it or not, we were moderate in our celebrations that night – an ice bath is a pretty effective party-stopper – but maybe I shouldn't have been so strict with myself, because the next morning I went out with big plans but couldn't repeat the magic. When Warney came in to bat the 'G went off and he certainly didn't disappoint, racking up a healthy 40 not out; before picking up another two wickets in England's final dig. There were a lot of unforgettable moments in that Test, but as he stood before that crowd and dipped his cap, well, that will live with me forever. We won't see his like again for a very long time.

If Warney's triumphant performance is my lasting memory from Melbourne, Justin Langer's swansong absolutely stole the show in Sydney. I really wanted him to be not out in the second innings so he and Haydos could walk off as winners together; they managed it and the footage proves it brought the house down. I knew it was Warney and Pidge's last Test too, but it was different with them. Shane had given us time to deal with it and Glenn was going onto the World Cup, so we'd all have a few more chances to say goodbye. This was the end of the road for Lang.

The raw emotion that I'd felt in Melbourne was replaced by a feeling of satisfied delirium in Sydney. I had a bowl but didn't get any wickets, and succumbed to Monty again in our first dig for 48. I still had a long way to go, but I was pretty sure I hadn't let anyone down this time around.

As if things couldn't get any better, we were invited by James Packer to a post-match shindig on his magnificent 32-metre yacht. Talk about generosity. It was far and away the best tinny on the

Harbour and I'll confess that I convinced the captain to take me on a little tour – just so I could see what I was missing. I looked into every room and checked out the engines … you could tell the boat tragics among us afterwards. The hospitality that night was sensational, the guest list about as tidy as you could imagine. The celebrations were pretty savage and went on till the wee hours, but everyone got themselves up and at it as usual in the morning.

The season had only stopped for a few hours but we were on the road again. As has been the case for as long as I have been around this game, I don't exactly know where that road is taking me, but I intend to keep on it as long as I can.

CHAPTER 19

MY GOLDFIELD ASHES XI

Rather than list my all-time-favourite World XI or my favourite team-mates since I began playing, I thought I'd do something a little closer to my heart. There's been a real surge in popularity over the past few years for 'fantasy' competitions – cricket, footy, just about any sport really – and it got me thinking … My fantasy competition wouldn't be just any old game, mind you; it'd be the mighty Goldfield Ashes in Charters Towers. The 'Ashes' have been held over the Australia Day long weekend since 1949 and feature the sort of cricket where you need to have excellent skills and sense of awareness, because if you stuff up and spill your beer, you have to wait until the next drinks break to go off and get another one from the esky. Of course if you lose the match, you can always get out of cooking the BBQ for the victors by challenging them to a winner-cooks-all game of touch footy. But that's another story.

The Goldfield Ashes are a gruelling test of a player, and many a young man has gone too hard, too soon and not lasted the distance. You need special qualities to succeed and more than just 12 players to win, so I've made my fantasy selection a proper squad. I've drawn from a wide talent pool but have also made a few key recruits. The only constraint I've put on myself as cricket supremo is that they all come from within Australia, well, more or less. It'd be fun to include the likes of Brian Lara, Freddie Flintoff, Darren Gough, Murali Muralitharan, Robbie Keys, Mark Ealham, Jack Russell and Sachin Tendulkar (actually that's a pretty fair team) … but I'm going to stick to my guns.

As you'll see, the squad has a few distinct elements, but every player has been chosen for a reason. So here we go:

Gorden Tallis

Darren Lockyer

Allan Langer

Wally Lewis

Trevor Gillmeister

THE LEAGUE BOYS. They're in mainly so we'd have a head start over any opposition in the touch footy stakes. Of course, having blokes nicknamed 'The Axe' (Gillmeister) and 'The Raging Bull' (Gordy Tallis) can't hurt if things get a bit heated in the North Queensland sun.

Yogi (Anthony Fortini)

Mick (Michael Sheehan)

Erk (Greg Erkkila)

Billy (Bill Hobbs)

THE NORTH QUEENSLANDERS – Yogi, my mate who has a property at Stone River near Ingham; Mick, who runs Esmeralda Station in the gulf country; Erk, who has a property at Abergowie and Billy, who owns a cattle and cane property that borders Yogi's place. They've been picked for the 'Bulls, Boars, Barra and Beer' training camp that I'd run prior to the Goldfield Ashes. As well as keeping us well supplied with fish and crabs, we've the added bonus that Mick has a helicopter so we're set if it rains and we need to dry the ground out in a hurry.

> **Gilly (Adam Gilchrist)**
>
> **Punter (Ricky Ponting)**
>
> **Pup (Michael Clarke)**
>
> **Mahbo (Jimmy Maher)**
>
> **Haydos (Matthew Hayden)**
>
> **Hopesy (James Hopes)**
>
> **Boof (Darren Lehmann)**
>
> **Kasper (Michael Kasprowicz)**
>
> **Bic (Andy Bichel)**
>
> **Pfaffy (Jeff Pfaff)**
>
> **Motty (Matthew Mott)**
>
> **Warney (Shane Warne)**

THE CRICKETERS – well, we've got to win a few games after all, haven't we? But each of these blokes brings a little something extra. Even though his knees won't enjoy it, Gilly will 'keep, and Punter can lead the side; Pup has learned to hunt recently so we could use some fresh legs; Mahbo's the comic relief and back-up 'keeper (he'll love that); Hopesy is the 'Fizzmaster' because he can't sit still, is a great bloke to have on tour and will bowl all day if we need him to; and Boof can win a game on any surface – turf, concrete, synthetic grass, ant bed, rolled mud, slashed mulga – which will come in handy, especially if we draw some of the outer grounds. I've picked Bic and Kasper because they can bowl all day too and will give us a bit of touch footy depth. And of course Bic's a dab hand on the BBQ, and Haydos will bring his cookbooks. Pfaffy and Motty are all-rounders in the truest sense – handy on the paddock and handy off it, no matter what the situation. And Pfaffy is an accountant as well so he'll look after the touring budget. I've taken a punt on Warney because I think the conditions will negate him a little, but we can always park him under a shady tree and bring him out when the sun sets.

Stevo (Steve Kelly)

Cooky (David Cook)

Rupert (Jason McCall)

Boxy (Darren Box)

THE SOUTH QUEENSLANDERS – Stevo is a plant operator from Ormeau and one of my mates from the Shearers Arms Hotel, so he'll come in handy if we need to do any running repairs on the grounds, or even carve one out of the bush in a hurry. And fittingly, he doesn't mind a beer either. Cooky has contacts galore throughout the world so will be our Mr Fix-it; and Rupert is a poet, former rugby player and one-time King of the Gabba Hill who fielded for the Bulls in an emergency, so will fit in on a number of fronts as our utility player.

He's been earmarked to write some stirring verse to psyche us up for the big games as well. Boxy is a Jacobs Well boy who has a sand-blasting business, and loves the outdoors like me. He's also a handyman and another good bush mechanic who's pulled me out of a few tight spots in our time.

Heidi Klum

Natalie Imbruglia

Malcolm Douglas

Kevin Costner

THE SPECIAL PROJECTS TEAM, aka The Imports. I'm not sure if Heidi is 100 per cent ready for this level of cricket, but I reckon she'll fit in and everyone will make her welcome. Truth is I've always been a bit of a fan. Ditto for Natalie, and I like her singing as well. We might need a bit of bushcraft where we're going so Mal will come in handy: you need someone who can turn their hand to almost anything in a tight spot. Finally Kevin Costner. Now this is where the 'fantasy' side of things steps up (as if Heidi and Natalie weren't enough of a giveaway). I chose Kev for a few reasons: firstly, because he's got a great voice and he'd be a terrific bloke to have around the campfire at night. He's bound to have a few stories and because he's directed movies, he'd handle a managerial function within our squad. He's got a pretty fair arm too (check out *Bull Durham, Field of Dreams* and *For The Love of the Game*), can ride a horse and shoot (*Dances With Wolves*) and can play a bit of golf (*Tin Cup*) which would be useful on the days off.

The squad's strong in a number of areas. There's almost a First XI of Fizz in there for starters, and I think we might have to run a bit of beer off a couple of them in the pre-season before we get serious. The cricket side of things is well covered with the blend of talent and champions, while the League boys would give us a nice solid foundation when it comes to the footy, the odd scuffle and some good old fashioned dry humour.

Now if I can just work out when we can all get together …

ROY'S HIGHEST SCORES
TWENTY20

02/07/2004
20/20, KENT v MIDDLESEX, MAIDSTONE

RUNS	BALLS	6's	STK-RT
112	43	3	260.46

16/06/2003
20/20, KENT v HAMPSHIRE, BECKENHAM

RUNS	BALLS	6's	STK-RT
96	37	3	259.45

18/07/2005
20/20, LANCASHIRE v DERBYSHIRE, MANCHESTER

RUNS	BALLS	6's	STK-RT
57	37	3	154.05

09/01/2006
20/20, AUSTRALIA v SOUTH AFRICA, BRISBANE

RUNS	BALLS	6's	STK-RT
54*	26	2	207.69

30/07/2005
20/20, LANCASHIRE v SURREY, THE OVAL

RUNS	BALLS	6's	STK-RT
52	30	1	173.33

SPELL 'CAT'

By Andrew Symonds

I reckon this book proves I'm a good sport but I do need to set the record straight when it comes one area close to my heart – spelling. Over the years, my team-mates – in particular Motty and Wade Seccombe – have subjected me to a number of gruelling tests. The first time, Motty came up with things like 'cat', 'dog', 'knife' (had to think about that for a sec), before hitting me with 'chimney'. Now Mum comes from Birmingham and had a pretty strong 'Brummie' accent when I was younger, and for whatever reason, I used to hear chimney as 'chimly' and so whenever I tried to spell it, an 'l' or an 'er' would creep in. The boys would be in hysterics as I kept crossing out my failed attempts and starting again, each time trying to find a way of including 'l' or 'er'. I refused to believe them at first, and Motty reckons I'm still suspicious that it isn't a worldwide conspiracy to wind me up.

Anyway, the spelling bee resurfaced on the 2005 tour of New Zealand for the Chappell-Hadlee Trophy. I was more confident they weren't going to catch me out, but the first word they threw up was 'pterodactyl'! I wasn't going to cop that so I got them to go around the room and see if anyone else could spell it. I'm happy to report that only one person knew it started with a 'p' and not a 't'. For once when it came to spelling, I had the last larf.

ANDREW SYMONDS CAREER

BORN 9 June 1975 Birmingham, West Midlands (England)
Right hand batsman
Right arm offspin/medium bowler

TEST CAREER
DEBUT 2003/04 Australia v Sri Lanka, Galle

M	INN	NO	RUNS	50	100	AVE	CT	OVERS	MDNS	RUNS	WKTS	AVE
10	15	–	286	2	–	19.07	10	149.0	33	409	9	45.44

HIGHEST SCORE 72   Australia v South Africa, Melbourne, 2005/06
BEST BOWLING 3/50 Australia v South Africa, Melbourne, 2005/06

FIRST-CLASS FOR QUEENSLAND

M	INN	NO	RUNS	50	100	AVE	CT	OVERS	MDNS	RUNS	WKTS	AVE
90	148	11	5329	20	14	38.90	53	1254.4	348	3591	107	33.56

HIGHEST SCORE 163   Queensland v South Australia, Adelaide, 2005/06
BEST BOWLING 4/39   Queensland v Western Australia, Perth, 1998/99

OTHER FIRST-CLASS AND COUNTY CRICKET

M	INN	NO	RUNS	50	100	AVE	CT	OVERS	MDNS	RUNS	WKTS	AVE
109	185	19	8061	35	26	48.56	81	1298.1	264	4249	105	40.47

HIGHEST SCORE 254*   Gloucestershire v Glamorgan, Abergavenny, 1995
BEST BOWLING 6/105   Kent v Sussex, Tunbridge Wells, 2002

FIRST-CLASS CAREER
DEBUT 1994/95 Queensland v New South Wales, Sydney

M	INN	NO	RUNS	50	100	AVE	CT	OVERS	MDNS	RUNS	WKTS	AVE
198	329	28	12819	53	38	42.59	141	2568.5	619	7703	211	36.51

HIGHEST SCORE 254*   Gloucestershire v Glamorgan, Abergavenny, 1995
BEST BOWLING 6/105   Kent v Sussex, Tunbridge Wells, 2002

COURTESY: ROSS DUNDAS

INTERNATIONAL LIMITED-OVERS CAREER
DEBUT 1998/99 Australia v Pakistan, Lahore

M	INN	NO	RUNS	50	100	AVE	STK-RT	CT	OVERS	MDNS	RUNS	WKTS	AVE
146	116	22	3697	18	5	39.33	92.22	65	837.1	27	4148	114	36.39

HIGHEST SCORE 156   Australia v New Zealand, Wellington, 2005/06
BEST BOWLING 5/18   Australia v Bangladesh, Manchester, 2005

AUSTRALIAN DOMESTIC LIMITED-OVERS CAREER
DEBUT 1993/94 Queensland v South Australia, Adelaide

M	INN	NO	RUNS	50	100	AVE	STK-RT	CT	OVERS	MDNS	RUNS	WKTS	AVE
65	61	8	1547	9	–	29.19	97.54	30	265.1	11	1263	36	35.08

HIGHEST SCORE 91   Queensland v Western Australia, Brisbane, 2001/02
BEST BOWLING 3/32   Queensland v Tasmania, Hobart, 1997/98

LIMITED-OVERS CAREER

M	INN	NO	RUNS	50	100	AVE	CT	OVERS	MDNS	RUNS	WKTS	AVE
360	320	40	9452	51	8	33.75	160	1740.5	68	8227	258	31.88

HIGHEST SCORE 156   Australia v New Zealand, Wellington, 2005/06
BEST BOWLING 6/14   Australia A v India A, Los Angeles, 1999/00

INTERNATIONAL TWENTY20 CAREER
DEBUT 1993/94 Queensland v South Australia, Adelaide

M	INN	NO	RUNS	50	100	AVE	STK-RT	CT	OVERS	MDNS	RUNS	WKTS	AVE
3	3	1	86	1	–	43.00	209.75	1	10.0	–	73	5	14.60

HIGHEST SCORE 54*   Australia v South Africa, Brisbane, 2005/06
BEST BOWLING 2/14   Australia v England, Southampton, 2005

COURTESY: ROSS DUNDAS

ACKNOWLEDGMENTS

For a first book, I can think of few better subjects to tackle than Andrew Symonds. He's a distinct individual and his story is by turns intriguing, compelling and a touch controversial. During the time I've known him, Roy has never sought the limelight, preferring instead to withdraw to the bush or the bay as soon as he was out of the cricketing spotlight, but since committing to this project, he has not showed the slightest reticence at laying bare his life. I thank him from the outset for his generosity and loyalty in putting faith in a first-time collaborator and for being such a willing participant.

In a similar vein, I express my deepest gratitude to John Buchanan, Adam Dale, Matthew Mott, Jimmy Maher, Michael Kasprowicz, Matthew Hayden, Michael Clarke, Jim Hunter, Toot Byron, Eric Adams, Terry Oliver, Justin Sternes, Joe Dawes, Trevor Hohns, Jack Russell, Mark Ealham, Robert Key, Jonathon Rose, Anthony Fortini and Brooke Marshall for making themselves available to talk about all things 'Roy'.

Ken and Barbara Symonds were a writer's dream, providing an encyclopaedic chronology, a wealth of wonderful family photos, generous insight and advice, and rigorous proofreading, all in the same package! Thank you for your devotion to the project.

I enjoyed great support from my workmates at Queensland Cricket, especially Graham Dixon and Andrew Blucher who gave the green light to tackle it when I first broached the subject; and welcome encouragement from my fellow State Media Managers and the Public Affairs team at Cricket Australia. My appreciation to Robert Craddock, Paul Malone, Ben Dorries, Peter Blucher and Ian Eckersley for their advice and enthusiasm, especially in the early days when my ignorance of what I was getting into would have filled a volume in itself.

On the same note, sincere thanks to Sandy Grant and the team at Hardie Grant Books – Keiran Rogers, Fran Berry and Megan Taylor – but especially Rod Morrison, who had to juggle the demanding roles of editor and sounding-board for a rookie writer, and never once let a note of panic creep into his voice or emails, even as deadlines loomed large. Glad you don't spook easily, Rod! Thanks also to the unsung heroes – the transcribers who filtered my gibbering questions and unprompted asides to deliver clean and readable copy to make the writing process so much easier; and to Chris Ryan, who like a master jeweller, provided polish and flourish where it was most needed.

A special thank-you to family and friends, especially those who provided valuable back-up around home when I was absenting myself to write. Coming from a family that has strong ties to the game, it has been both enjoyable and rewarding to be part of a book that will hopefully strike a chord with lovers of exciting cricket.

My wife Cheryl provided wise counsel, judicious encouragement and much needed time, especially when I had made less than optimal use of that originally available to me. I look forward to returning the favours when you write your book one day! And to our sons, Darcy and Tim, I hope there's a 'Roy' around for you to enjoy when you both get a bit bigger – take it from me, it's a lot of fun!

Stephen Gray,
September 2006

Those who know me well will know that books and I have been infrequent acquaintances throughout much of my life. Not that I dislike reading or anything – it was just a bit 'indoors' for me – and despite growing up with a pair of schoolteachers for parents, I always seemed to find something else outside that I would rather be doing. So getting to the point where a book about me is available for others to read is a decent sort of leap.

I'll confess it was not something that was on my mind until my manager Matt Fearon suggested we might look at going down that path. Now we've arrived, I'm delighted to be able to thank the people who made it happen and those whose friendship and guidance have helped me get to where I am today. There are a lot of them and most are featured in the book in some way or another. Still, I'll have a crack at handing out a few well-deserved wraps.

Matt and the team at Octagon – your passion drove this project from the outset. Thanks for your advice and support through the rough and the smooth.

Sandy, Rod, Megan and everyone at Hardie Grant Books: thank you all for making me feel welcome and convincing me that what I was doing would be a good thing and that people would be interested in reading about me.

I dedicated this book to my family and it goes without saying that without Mum and Dad, there wouldn't be anything like this to show for it. I probably don't tell you enough, so thanks for giving me such a great grounding in life. My family has always been essential to me and that was brought home in July 2006 when my Grandad died suddenly in Ballarat. We'd only just shared some fresh muddies a few weeks earlier and I will feel his loss keenly this summer.

This seems a bit like the Oscars so before a band strikes up and I have to exit, stage left, there's a huge extended group of people I'd like to acknowledge.

A special thank-you to my co-author Stephen Gray. I hope you look back on this with fond memories, Earl – I enjoyed it and that probably says it all. I appreciate the hard work you did and the sacrifices you and your family made along the way. Cheers, mate!

To all my team-mates, both past and present, with the Australian team, the Queensland Bulls and the Gold Coast Dolphins. I can't name you all, but thanks, boys, I wouldn't swap the experiences we've had for anything.

My coaches over the years at club, state and national level: you've all played a role, whether small or large, in shaping me as an individual. Likewise the staff at Queensland Cricket: nothing is too much trouble and they've made my life easier over the years, even if on the flipside, I've made their lives a bit harder sometimes. Thanks!

Finally, my mates in North Queensland and around home at Ormeau and the Gold Coast. Thanks for always keeping me in touch with who I am, for being so generous with your time, and for being great mates. May there be plenty more adventures ahead.

Andrew Symonds,
September 2006

PHOTOGRAPHY CREDITS

Front cover courtesy William West/AFP/Getty Images, Kristian Dowling/Getty Images; back cover and page 240 courtesy Florian Groehn; page x courtesy Ryan Pierse/Getty Images; pages 6, 9, 12, 15, 16, 19, 20, 23, 27, 32, 37, 39, 43, 44, 46, 48, 53, 60, 70, 73, 75, 116, 206, 216 and 219 courtesy the Symonds family; page 34 courtesy Brett Costello/NewsPix; page 56, 58, 76, 93, 94, 164 and 166 courtesy Duane Hart/Sporting Images; pages 63 and 64 courtesy the Mott family; pages 78, 194 and 210 courtesy AFP/NewsPix; pages 84, 104, 111, 130 and 178 courtesy Sporting Images; pages 86, 118, 126, 142, 146, 176, 202 and 232 courtesy Queensland Cricket; page 96 courtesy Phil Hillyard Cricket/NewsPix; page 220 courtesy William West/AFP/Getty Images.